market **vegetarian**

market **vegetarian**

easy **organic** recipes
for every occasion

Ross Dobson

photography by Richard Jung

RYLAND
PETERS
& SMALL

LONDON NEW YORK

Dedication

This book is dedicated to all those passionate and hard working local market farmers who provide us with a guarantee of the provenance of our fresh fruit and vegetables.

Design and Photographic Art Direction
 Steve Painter
Senior Editor Julia Charles
Production Manager Patricia Harrington
Art Director Leslie Harrington
Publishing Director Alison Starling

Food Stylist Ross Dobson
Prop Stylist Róisín Nield
Indexer Hilary Bird

First published in the United States
in 2008
by Ryland Peters & Small, Inc.
519 Broadway, 5th Floor
New York, NY 10012
www.rylandpeters.com

10 9 8 7 6 5 4 3

Text © Ross Dobson 2008
Design and photographs
© Ryland Peters & Small 2008

Library of Congress Cataloging-in-Publication Data

Dobson, Ross, 1965-
  Market vegetarian : easy organic recipes for every occasion / Ross Dobson ; photography by Richard Jung. -- 1st ed.
    p. cm.
  Includes index.
  ISBN 978-1-84597-720-7
  1. Vegetarian cookery. 2. Natural foods. I. Title.

TX837.D58 2008
641.5'636--dc22

2008018052

Printed and bound in China

Notes

• All spoon measurements are level unless otherwise stated.

• Eggs are large unless otherwise specified. Uncooked or partially cooked eggs should not be served to the very old, frail, young children, pregnant women, or those with compromised immune systems.

Author's Acknowledgments

It is a privilege to be given the opportunity to create yet another beautiful book with Ryland Peters & Small. Thank you to Alison for your ongoing confidence in me—I look forward to our dinners in London. To Julia, whose editorial queries appear like magic across the vast distance between London and Sydney. Thank you for keeping me on my toes and not missing a trick. Thanks also go to Richard for his beautiful photography—it's always such a pleasure to work with you. And to Steve who always makes such a perfect job of the design. Last, but not least, Róisín whose beautiful props really do make our work so much easier. Thank you all so much.

contents

farmers' markets: one degree of separation

In my view good vegetarian cooking is not about reinventing the wheel—the world is already full of wonderful vegetable dishes that I look to for my inspiration. My ethos is to choose quality ingredients, understand the classic flavor combinations, and introduce a twist or two to keep things modern and interesting. I should also say that this is not a cookbook exclusively for vegetarians (and it is at this point that I must confess to not being a vegetarian myself). But I am no less discerning about what I choose to buy, cook, and eat. I want to be assured that I'm being offered the very best ingredients and it always puts my mind at ease to know where my food has come from.

You may be passionate about the source of your food for ethical or health reasons, or you may just want the freshest and best produce because you enjoy eating well. These days the provenance of what we eat is relevant to everyone and is a highly topical and hotly debated issue. It may seem as if it's only recently that we have become so interested in where our food comes from but for some people it has been a concern for a long time. In parts of the United States the resurgence in fresh food shopping options, such as farmers' markets, began in the early 1970s, but it has really only been in the last decade that this movement has gained momentum in other developed countries. There is now a widespread desire to know where our food originates from and many chefs and food writers, myself included, are only too happy to champion the cause.

Today's globalized food market ensures that most of our food can be bought all year round but the obvious problem with buying fruit and vegetables during the months when they do not grow locally is that they have, inevitably, had to travel a considerable distance to reach the shelves of your local grocer. This means that they have had to be harvested or picked early and before they have had a chance to ripen as nature intended. The ripening process is then stopped in its tracks by refrigerated transport and other forms of high-technology food storage. Not surprisingly, by the time you put the "fresh" fruit and vegetables in your shopping cart they are often lacking in flavor and can be a big disappointment. Market researchers have established that modern consumers like to see the word "fresh" on food packaging so it's a term that's often used but rarely true. "Fresh" shelled peas in a plastic tray and covered in plastic wrap are already well past their prime—fresh in this case simply means not frozen. You probably won't even see the word fresh used to describe produce on sale at your local farmers' market; it would be both preaching to the converted and superfluous—of course what's on sale there is fresh!

We may think of the concept of a farmers' market as being a relatively new thing but in many countries around the world the fresh food markets have been a way of life for centuries. I've been lucky enough to see baskets of just-picked, exotic herbs on display at the Aw Taw Kaw markets in Bangkok, daily harvested squash blossoms at the Campo dei Fiori in Rome and squeaky fresh corn-on-the-cob at an Amish stall in Union Square in New York City. True, these are unique and famous marketplaces, and for most of us they are a long way from home, but they are essentially no different to your local market. Whether in the heart of a massive metropolis or the parking lot of your local school, they all share the same philosophy and purpose. They are a direct link between the grower and the buyer and a place where only one degree of separation exists between you and the origin of your food. The stalls at your local food market are more often than not manned by the growers themselves and they become the guarantors of the provenance of the food you buy there. The weekend is often the only time that they are not in the fields or orchards and for some it's their only day off. Even so, some of the stallholders would have been up since the early hours of the morning gathering, packing, and preparing their produce for its trip to the market—the evidence will be the dirt on their hands. These people are dedicated to growing food with care and concern for the environment and respect for the seasons. This, in turn, has a positive effect on the quality of the food you buy. I do believe that the resulting produce is vastly superior to that which is produced using methods that meet a financial bottom line or grown on a huge, unnatural scale to meet consumer demand.

The other main problem with a globalized market is that it has also gradually and systematically eliminated local producers and in doing so has also diminished many of the unique foods and flavors that were at one time available to us. In being denied a choice of quality produce it seems we have also been alienated from our kitchens. The lack of varieties and types of veggies available at the supermarket has resulted in limited cooking styles, techniques, and methods. Supporting your local farmers' market will not only have a positive impact on local farming economies but ultimately guarantee the diversity of food available to us over the years to come—surely an investment worth the return. Okay, so the farmers' market may not be as convenient as a supermarket. It might be tough to find parking, but you could walk. It might be raining, but you could carry an umbrella. The food might be dirty but this ensures a greater level of intimacy with the food as you have to spend time washing and preparing it yourself. It might only be open one or two days per week but who wants to go shopping more than that anyway? The process is slower and more relaxed. For me, the market becomes a place to escape from the fast pace of modern life and when it comes to food I'm all for slowing things down a little. It's so much fun to go to a local market, meet the growers and talk to them about their produce—in my experience they are only too happy to talk to you and offer advice on what variety of potato or type of mushroom is best suited to your purpose. You may also run into your friends and neighbors so seize the opportunity to have a relaxed chat and even exchange some recipe ideas for all the wonderful things you have just put in your basket. No fluorescent lights, no piped muzak, no shopping carts, and food encased in plastic. In this fast-paced modern world the marketplace is where we can indulge in a little nostalgia for a more traditional way of life.

The most colorful and exciting stalls at any farmers' market are undoubtedly the fruit and vegetable ones. They are a theater of color and every few weeks, as the curtain closes on one class act it opens on another. We drift through the fresh, green days of early spring, when pickings are relatively slim, but we have shoots and stems such as asparagus and forced rhubarb to keep us entertained. We gradually see the arrival of the peas, beans, and pods of late spring and then the jewel-like vine fruits of summer, including my personal favorite, the tomato. Tender summer squashes and leafy salad vegetables are gradually replaced on the stalls by early fall produce in hues that define the season; deep purple eggplants, blood-red plums, rust-colored pumpkins, and butternut squash. And so it continues throughout the year—plentiful, organically grown, seasonal food, at its best.

In developing the recipes for this book I focused on what I feel like eating at different times of the week or on different occasions. I like nothing better than enjoying a bottle of wine and sharing a plate of food with friends so I've included a selection of my favorite little dishes, dips, and parcels—all just right for grazing and relaxed entertaining. On weekdays I want to eat well but I don't want to spend too long getting my food ready because of other demands on my time. What is needed is good food fast—some tomatoes warmed in a little olive oil, their sweetness offset with a handful of bitter radicchio, and tossed through my favorite pasta—basically midweek meals that are easier done than said! It is on Saturdays that I am truly inspired. For many of us folks dedicated to buying our produce locally, this is market day. I stock up on great, fresh ingredients in the morning and have the rest of the day free to spend in my kitchen. I find it a comforting, meditative place to be and my idea of heaven is being enveloped in the aroma of freshly-baked pumpkin soda bread as I experiment, creating new dishes with all the goodies I've procured that day. Some ingredients lend themselves to simply being thrown into a pot with a few herbs (the alchemy of one-pot cooking) so I've devoted a chapter to soups and stews. I also have a sweet tooth so could not resist including some treats but they are all developed around seasonal fruits so you need not feel too guilty—you can quite literally have your cake and eat it!

know your onions: buying market produce

Here you'll find some useful tips on what to look for when out shopping and how to store your produce to keep it at its best. I find it easier to categorize vegetables and fruit by how I use them in the kitchen rather than strictly by their botanical family, so that's what I've done here.

root vegetables and winter squashes

potato sweet potato celeriac parsnip turnip rutabaga carrot beets pumpkin squash

These are the dirty boys of the market—the vegetables that grow close to or underneath the ground. They are generally most abundant and at their peak during the cooler months.

Arguably the most popular is the humble **potato**. Hailing originally from South America, it was introduced to Europe by the early explorers of the New World. There are more than 400 varieties in existence, though most of these are not widely available. They come in so many shapes, colors, and sizes that buying what you need can be confusing. To simplify matters, there are really only two main types of potato—waxy and floury. Waxy potatoes tend to be young, new potatoes. They are less starchy and stay firm making their flesh best for recipes where you want your potato to hold its shape such as the Taleggio and Potato Tortilla (see page 35). Floury potatoes, usually maincrop, are more starchy so they bake, roast, mash, and fry well—perfect for Crispy Oven Wedges (see page 22). When buying any sort of potato avoid any that seem withered, have damp patches or are sprouting. New potatoes should ideally be eaten within 2–3 days but maincrop potatoes will keep for several months in a dark, cool, dry place. **Sweet potatoes** have a distinctive sugary flavor and are excellent baked, mashed, roasted, or used in soups such as my Sweet Potato and Coconut Soup (see page 79). When buying sweet potatoes do choose small ones as the larger ones can be rather fibrous. They will keep in a dark, cool, dry place for about 8 days. **Celeriac** is actually the root of a variety of celery and has a similar, though milder, flavor. When grated and eaten raw it's crunchy but when cooked its texture is more like potato. Choose firm and smooth vegetables, still with their tops on, which should be fresh and lively looking. They will keep for a few days in a dark, cool place. **Parsnips** were widely used throughout the Middle Ages before the potato had been introduced. They are related to carrots and similarly sweet and delicious—try the Roasted Parsnip and Garlic Dip (see page 18). Choose small or medium-sized ones that feel firm and don't have any sprouting roots. **Turnips** and **rutabagas** are close relatives as both belong to the cabbage family. Turnips have a distinctive peppery flavor, while

rutabagas are more earthy and sweeter. Buy the youngest, smallest ones you can find, ideally with fresh green tops. The orange **carrots** we know and love today originally came from Holland, but up until the Middle Ages all carrots were purple! Growers often delight in such oddities and you might be lucky enough to find some at your local farmers' market. All vegetables have a better flavor if they are grown organically, but this is particularly true of carrots. Look for bunches of young, tapered, pencil-thin ones that still have their feathery tops attached. For a real treat bake the Carrot and Walnut Cake on page 146. Glorious **beets** have been eaten since Roman times. Delicious when roasted, boiled or simply sliced into wedges and added to salads—see my Home-made Cheese with Roasted Baby Beets, Fennel, and Pine Nuts on page 106. Always buy small baby beets which have their whiskers intact and at least 2 inches of leaf stalk at the top; if they are too closely cropped they will bleed during cooking. They will keep for several weeks in a cool place. **Winter squashes** lend themselves to the same cooking styles and flavorings as root veggies so I've included them here. There are a huge number of varieties and to add to the confusion, many are known by several different names. The most famous is of course **pumpkin** with its sweet, slightly honeyed flavor that works perfectly in my Orange Vegetable and Scallion Pilau (see page 75). Other popular squashes include the pear-shaped **butternut**, a reliable everyday variety that will work in pretty much any recipe that calls for squash. Try the Spaghetti with Butternut Squash, Sage, and Pecorino on page 60. Try to buy them firm and unblemished with smooth skins. All winter squashes can be stored for long periods in a cool place.

green vegetables

spinach swiss chard cauliflower broccoli savoy cabbage kale collards bok-choy

Greens of one sort or another are available throughout the year. It seems that whenever one finishes, another one comes into season.

Spinach is arguably the most versatile of all the green veggies. Almost every cuisine around the world features it in some form or other from Italy to the Middle East. I like to cook a nutritious Baked Spinach Mornay (see page 122) as a brunch dish. It grows all year round and you'll have no difficulty buying it fresh so don't settle for tired or floppy stalks. It will keep in the fridge for 1–2 days.

Swiss chard is similar to spinach but has bigger leaves and a stronger flavor—I use it to make a Swiss Chard, Feta Cheese, and Egg Pie (see page 126). Avoid buying any with withered leaves or flabby stems. Store in a cool place and eat within 3–4 days.
Cauliflower was introduced to Europe by the Moors who took it to Spain but it's thought to have come originally from China. I'm a big fan and keen to show how delicious it can be when it's cooked well—do try my Spiced Cauliflower with Red Bell Pepper and Peas (see page 79) or Cauliflower and Caperberries on Halloumi (see page 32). When choosing your cauliflower look out for a creamy white and unblemished head with outer leaves that curl tightly around it. Store it in a cool place for no longer than 1–2 days.
Broccoli is a relatively modern vegetable. It was developed in Italy from the now trendy purple sprouting broccoli. There is actually little to choose between them in taste so it's just a question of whether you prefer the compactness of a head or the leafiness of the sprouting variety. When buying it choose loose bundles, rather than pre-wrapped ones. It should be firm and make a cracking sound when the florets are snapped from the stem. Avoid any that look wilted or have damaged flowerheads. A head of broccoli will keep in the fridge for 2–3 days. Check out my Spaghetti with Broccoli, Walnuts, and Ricotta on page 53. There are many varieties of cabbage but all share the same unfortunate problem of a rank smell and flavor if overcooked so the trick is not to overcook them!
Savoy cabbage, with its crimped or curly leaves has a mild flavor and is particularly tender, hence its popularity. **Collards** are a very popular vegetable in the Southern States, grown during Summer and Fall for harvesting in Spring. Dark and leafy **kale** and **curly kale** are not cabbages but a variety of brassica (as is the Chinese green **bok-choy**) and have a minerally taste, similar to broccoli, that I love. Avoid buying cabbages or greens that look or feel puffy and they should keep in a cool place for several days.

salad greens
iceberg red leaf oak leaf romaine arugula watercress Belgian endive radicchio escarole curly endive

Salad greens are hugely popular today and there are plenty to choose from. Some are lettuces, while others belong to vegetable families—what they have in common is that they are eaten raw and often what we crave in the warmer summer months.

Round lettuces are sold in heads. Butterheads are the classic "Peter Rabbit" kitchen garden lettuces with floppy loosely packed leaves—perfect for the Old-fashioned Garden Salad on page 43. Crispheads, such as **iceberg**, have a nice crunch but not such a great flavor. Looseheads are non-hearting lettuces with loose leaves and these include **red leaf** and **oak leaf**. They don't have the best flavor but do look fantastic in your salad bowl! **Romaine** lettuce comes originally from the Greek islands where it was found by the Romans. It is generally considered to be the most delicious lettuce because of its firm texture and faintly nutty and sweet flavor. It's the must-have ingredient for an authentic Caesar salad. As well as lettuce there are a number of other salad leaves—**arugula** being the trendiest. Its hot, peppery taste adds a flavor kick to any salad.
Watercress is probably the most pungent of all the salad leaves and has a distinctly raw flavor. Just a few sprigs will perk up a mixture of milder-tasting leaves and it makes a deliciously peppery soup (see Watercress and Pea Soup on page 96). **Belgian endive** (also known as French endive, chicory and witlof), **radicchio**, and **escarole** are close relatives and share a similar taste. Chicory can be eaten raw but are often baked, stir-fried, or poached. Radicchio looks like a small head of lettuce and is the painted lady of the salad leaf world with its deep wine-red leaves and striking cream ribs. Again it can be eaten raw or as a hot vegetable but does lose it's gorgeous color when cooked. **Curly endive**, also known as frisée looks pretty and delicate because of its frilly leaves but actually has a rather bitter taste so is better mixed with milder salad leaves. At farmers' markets salad greens are often sold in bags or bunches or even buckets and barrels so that you can help yourself. Do look out for mesclun (from the French mescla meaning "to mix") a nifty salad mix of assorted small young leaves which often includes oak leaf, radicchio, curly endive, baby spinach, and arugula. The leaves can be simply tossed in a light, lemony dressing or a mustardy vinaigrette. Avoid buying any salad greens that are limp, wilted, or shiny. Keep round lettuces wrapped in dampened paper towels in the fridge. Wash loose leaves in water (do not soak) and dry them very well. Store them in the fridge in a clean, sealed plastic bag.

peas, beans, and pods
garden peas fava beans green beans corn

Probably the first vegetables to be cultivated by man, peas and beans have been found in settlements from the late Stone Age onwards. They were valuable to ancient man as they could be dried and stored, which meant that food was available all year round.

Garden peas are one of the delights of summer and are best when absolutely fresh. So, many "fresh" peas you see in plastic wrap at the supermarket are already past their best. Buy them still in their pods from a grower and enjoy them as soon as possible. **Fava beans** are one of man's earliest foods. They grow in most climates

and soils and were a staple food throughout the Dark Ages and Middle Ages and only replaced by the potato in the 17th and 18th centuries. As with peas, try to buy fava beans are fresh as possible and eat them as soon as you can. Pods should be small and tender and the beans nutty and sweet with skins that don't need to be removed. **Green beans**, also known as French beans and Haricots Verts belong to the same large and varied family as Thai beans and yellow wax beans. They are widely used in France and an essential ingredient in my Niçoise-style Brown Rice Salad on page 40. Beans should be bright and crisp. Avoid wilted ones, or those with overly mature pods which feel spongy when lightly squeezed. Green beans do not keep well so use as soon as possible after buying or picking them. Similarly, as soon as **corn** is picked, its sugar begins to turn to starch. The flavor fades and the kernels toughen so the quicker it goes from crop to pot the better! Look for husks that are clean and green with tassles which are golden with no sign of matting. The corn itself should look firm and plump. Don't keep husks too long—a day at most in the fridge. Try one of my recipes that's designed to showcase fresh corn at its best—Summer Corn Soup on page 66 or Corn Relish on page 36.

vegetable fruits and summer squashes

tomatoes bell peppers chiles eggplants zucchini

The "fruits" of the vegetable world are the most colorful, and most versatile, of all veggies. They are widely used throughout the world to add jewel-like color, flavor, and texture to all kinds of recipes.

Along with onions, **tomatoes** are arguably the most important fresh ingredient used in any kitchen, especially in the Mediterranean where they are absolutely essential. Used with garlic and olive oil, they create the basis of so many dishes that it's hard to find any in which they are not included! There are a staggering 7,000 varieties, ranging from beefsteak to cherry, and they range in color from bright red to vibrant yellow. Sadly many of these varieties are new hybrids, specially developed to be available all year round. I'm not a fan and have long lamented the availability of the bland year-round tomato, so it's good to see a resurgence in popularity of what I call "real" tomatoes—heirloom varieties that have been grown outdoors, on a vine planted in soil, and in the sunshine. When buying tomatoes first use your eyes then your nose. Overripe ones will smell a bit rancid, don't buy any that smell less than wonderful. Choose fruits that are firm and don't worry if they are underripe. In summer either keep them in a bowl or line them up on a sun-drenched windowsill to ripen but do not store them in the fridge.

The hybrid varieties never seem to ripen or for that matter go off which just can't be a good thing! **Bell peppers** and **chiles** are both members of the capsicum family. From a culinary point of view the only difference between them is their heat—chiles are hot and pungent and bell peppers are sweet and mild. Both can be eaten raw, stir-fried, grilled, or roasted and their shape makes them perfect for stuffing. Bell peppers are available in a range of colors, from green (the least mature with a fresh "raw" flavor) to red which are ripened green ones and much sweeter. When you buy peppers or chiles they should be glossy and firm—avoid any that look dull and wrinkled. They will keep for a few days in the fridge. I think the versatility of the **eggplant** is unsurpassed—they are grown and cooked all over the world and feature in a multitude of dishes. They are many varieties, according to their country of origin, ranging from cute little pea eggplants in Thailand to the glossy, dark purple zeppelin-shaped ones grown in the West. All have a similar bland yet smoky flavor and a flesh that is spongy when raw, but soft after cooking (see page 85 for my Eggplant, Tomato, and Red Lentil Curry). When buying eggplants choose ones that feel heavy and quite firm to the touch and have glossy, clear skins. They will keep well in the fridge for up to 2 weeks. **Zucchini** are the best-loved summer squash. They are quick to cook and tender with a delicate flavor. They should always be firm and glossy—avoid any that feel squashy or look limp. Choose small, young zucchini for the best flavor and if they still have their blossoms attached so much the better as they are delicious to eat—see the Baked Squash Blossoms on page 89.

shoots and stems

asparagus fennel celery artichoke

Vegetables in which the whole or part of the stalk is eaten are classified as shoots or stems. Some, like asparagus, are early season vegetables, others, such as the globe artichoke arrive later in the warmer summer months.

Unless you are lucky enough to grow your own **asparagus** it's definitely a luxury. Its price, even in season, sets it apart from other vegetables. The spears have an intensely savory flavor that's perfect with eggs (see Asparagus, Corn, and Goat Cheese Frittata on page 56) or pasta. Asparagus has a relatively short growing season from late spring to early summer. When buying asparagus the tips should be slightly furled and the stalks fresh and straight. It will keep for several days. It's best to untie the bundles and stand them in a pitcher of cold water in the fridge. **Fennel** is hugely popular in Italy where it is used raw, simply sliced into salads (see page 26) or oven-baked until tender. It has a pleasing aniseed flavor and the feathery fronds can be used like a herb to add flavor towards the end of cooking or as a garnish. Buy small tender bulbs—they should be clean and white with no bruises and the fronds should be green and lively. It will keep for a day or 2 in the fridge. **Celery** has also been added to salads for centuries for its sharp, distinctive flavor and crunchy texture. If possible buy unwashed white celery. It might look "dirty" but it has a better flavor than the pristine but rather bland green variety. Look for fresh-looking leaves and straight stems. It will keep for several days in the fridge but if limp it can be revived by wrapping it in paper towels and standing it in a pitcher of water as you would cut flowers. **Globe artichokes** are synonymous with summer and, like the heads of cauliflower and broccoli, they are the flower of an edible plant, in this case a thistle. Grilled as an antipasti, tossed into pasta, or whizzed up in a soup (such as the Globe Artichoke, Tarragon, and Roquefort soup on page 103) these photogenic vegetables are always a treat. At their best artichokes should be fresh, crisp, with a bloom on their leaves and the inner leaves wrapped tightly round the choke. They will keep for 2–3 days in the fridge but should be eaten as soon as possible after buying them.

pungent bulbs
onions shallots leeks garlic chives

Known as alliums, there are more than 300 distinct species in the onion family but only a handful are used for culinary purposes. Although there are some wild forms, most are cultivated but the one thing they all have in common is their pungent smell and flavor.

Alongside tomatoes, **onions** are almost certainly the most important ingredient in the kitchen. They can be used raw in salads, browned to give depth of flavor in a stew, or gently sautéed until soft and caramelized for a savory tart. Try both the Crispy Onion Rings on page 21 or the Slow-cooked Onion and Cider Soup on page 69 and you'll see just just how versatile they are! Onions will keep well stored in a cool, dry place but don't store them in the fridge as they will go soft. Scallions are simply early-maturing varieties of onion. They have a mild, sweet flavor with a fresh, green snap, which makes them good in salads, Asian-style stir-fries or used as a tasty garnish, as I've done with the Vegetable Potstickers with Orange Dipping Sauce on page 25. Unlike older onions they do not store well but can be kept for a few days in a cool place or the fridge but are best used really fresh. **Shallots** are distinct from onions as they grow in clusters of bulbs. They are also smaller and have finer layers as they contain less water. Shallots can be used much in the same way as onions but they are milder so are good for dishes where you want a more subtle flavor. They should be firm without any green shoots and will keep well for several months in a cool, dry place. **Leeks** have their own distinct flavor but are, again, a versatile

ingredient. They are wonderful in soups and broths, pies and casseroles, or simply braised. There are many varieties but little to choose between them in terms of flavor. They can range in size from tiny baby leeks that can be steamed whole as you would asparagus or larger tougher ones that need more cooking. Always buy crisp, firm leeks with perky green parts. **Garlic** is an ingredient few modern cooks, including me, would be without. It was at one time known rather unfairly as "stinking rose" and considered offensive and acrid. In today's kitchen its uses are infinite—softened in butter or oil as a base for risottos, pasta sauces, stews, soups, casseroles, and curries; roughly chopped and sizzled in hot oil for a few seconds in a stir-fry; or finely minced and used in a salad dressing. As a general rule the smaller the bulb, the stronger the flavor. Fresh, new-season garlic has a subtle, mild flavor so it's particularly good if you are using it raw. Garlic bulbs should be firm and round with clear, papery skins. Avoid any that are beginning to sprout. They are best stored in a cool, dry place as damp air will quickly turn the cloves to a grey powder. The aromatic stems of **chives** are used raw to add a faint onion flavor. Sprinkle them over egg dishes, soups, or pasta, or stir through sour cream or soft cheese to give it bite. Buy them green and firm, not too floppy and store them in the fridge for just a few days.

mushrooms
cremini cep morel chanterelle white brown portobello enokitake shiitake

You will often find a stall at the market specializing in mushrooms as there are so many edible varieties, both wild and cultivated.

Wild mushrooms are usually more expensive as they are seasonal and gathered by foragers. The most readily available are the wide and flat **cremini** mushrooms which are perfect for stuffing and baking (see Baked Mushrooms with Manchego Béchamel on page 26). Other more exclusive wild varieties you will see include **cep**, **morel** and **chanterelle**. All make an indulgent addition to soups and stews and are delicious with pasta (see Wild Mushroom Lasagne on page 129). Cultivated varieties include **white** (the very young ones are button mushrooms), **brown**, and the giant **portobello** which are delicious with pasta (see recipe on page 100). These are widely available most of the year as they are grown in subterranean conditions and thus unaffected by the changing seasons. Some Asian varieties are now cultivated including the cute little Japanese **enokitake** and popular **shiitake**. All mushrooms should be kept in paper bags in the fridge. Plastic bags or punnets will make them sweat and eventually they turn slippery and unappetizing. It's always best to eat them within 2–3 days.

summer stone fruits

peaches nectarines apricots plums cherries

These delicious fruits all grow on trees in summer and are soft and juicy with a single, central stone or pit. **Peaches** are sometimes known as "the queen of fruits" and it's not hard to see why. To me they are the perfect fresh fruit for eating raw. Their fuzz-free cousins **nectarines** are also deliciously irresistible. All stone fruits, especially **plums** and **apricots** respond well to being gently poached (see Coconut Creamed Rice with Poached Plums on page 152) and also work well in cakes as their juiciness keeps things moist (try the Upside-down Peach Cake on page 143). Unfortunately they don't travel well so try to buy stone fruit as near to where it has grown as possible. Once they are picked they will soften at room temperature but not ripen. Look for fruit at the market that smells ripe and gives slightly when gently pressed. All can be refrigerated in a paper bag for a few days. **Cherries** are one of the great delights of summer. Choose plump ones with shiny, unblemished skins. It's best to buy them still on the stalk which should be green and flexible, not dry and brown. Unwashed cherries will keep for a few days if refrigerated; it's best to wash them just before serving.

autumn orchard fruit

apples pears

The most popular of all fruits, the number of varieties of **apples** is enough to make your head spin. Apples can be divided into two groups—eating apples and pie apples—but there's considerable crossover. Braeburn, Jonathon, Gala, Honeycrisp, and Mutsu are all good for munching on as a healthy snack. Tarter pie apples such as Northern Spy, Granny Smith, Winesap,and Rhode Island Greening are best baked in pies and tarts. Sweet and fragrant McIntosh make the best apple sauce. Apples continue to ripen after being picked and if left too long they become mealy, floury, and unappetizing. Try to find just-picked fruit with stalks intact and dry, taut skin. Don't be seduced by the color of an apple's skin— thick, brilliant red, waxy skins often have woolly, tasteless flesh. Apples can be stored in the fridge or in a dark, cool, dry place. There are now almost as many varieties of **pears** as there are apples. (Try the Salad of Winter Fruit on page 43). They are more fragile than apples and deteriorate very quickly, becoming squashy and unpleasant. Test for ripeness by pressing gently; the fruit should give a little, but still be quite firm. Ripe pears can be stored in the fridge for a few days and unripened ones should be kept in a bowl at room temperature, where they will ripen in 2–3 days.

soft berries

strawberries raspberries blackberries

Whether wild or cultivated, fresh berries are always a treat and the best-flavored **strawberries** are sweet summer ones. There is something satisfying about foraging for your own berries so if you have the chance to do so give it a try. Sweetly intense **raspberries** are in fact a member of the rose family, as are **blackberries**, and, as such, are both more fragile than strawberries. It's best not to wash them as it ruins their texture. When buying any berries check that those at the bottom of the punnet are not damaged or moldy. Ideally berries should be eaten the day they are picked or bought but they will keep in the fridge, loosely covered, for not longer than 2 days. Remove from the fridge at least 1 hour before eating.

citrus fruits

lemons limes oranges

Citrus fruits are packed with juice and have a tough, bitter peel that contains aromatic oils. **Lemons** are always associated with Mediterranean-style cooking as they are one of the key flavorings used and are a kitchen essential for me. **Limes** have thinner, smoother skins and are also highly aromatic. Unlike lemons they grown in tropical regions and are an essential ingredient in Southeast Asian and Mexican cooking. **Oranges** are also valued for their fragrant zest and their blossoms. When buying any citrus fruit choose unwaxed, unblemished and firm fruits that feel heavy for their size as this tells you that they will be juicy. Mold forms quickly on all citrus fruit so keep them in a dry place; a fruit bowl is fine for a few days but in humid conditions keep them in the fridge and they should keep for up to 2 weeks.

rhubarb

Strictly speaking **rhubarb** is not a fruit, but a vegetable. It is too sour to eat raw but has a distinctive and delicious flavor when cooked and sweetened and is in its element when served with custard (see the Rhubarb and Custard Pots on page 140). Early forced rhubarb is vivid pink, tender and a real treat, so keep your eyes out for that at the market and by buying it you will probably be supporting a local industry. Later maincrop rhubarb is more tart but it's ideal for baking in a cake or crumble. When buying rhubarb go for crisp, firm, and bright stalks that release sap when you snap them. It can be stored for a few days in the fridge.

sharing plates

trio of vegetable dips with spelt toasts

Have you ever been lucky enough to share a plate of mixed dips at a Turkish restaurant? It's the vibrant colors that first grab my attention, quickly followed by the delicious flavors. These dips are all made with root vegetables, including the ubiquitous carrot, all too often lurking at the bottom of your veggie box. They all have a creamy texture, so the crisp spelt toasts make a nice nutty contrast.

roasted parsnip and garlic dip

2 tablespoons chilled butter
⅓ cup heavy cream
½ teaspoon sea salt
¼ teaspoon white pepper
1 lb. parsnips, peeled and sliced
1 garlic bulb, cut in half

Serves 6–8

Preheat the oven to 350°F. Lightly butter a small baking dish. Put the cream in a small bowl and stir in the salt and pepper.

Put the parsnips in the baking dish with the garlic. Pour the cream over the top, cover with foil and cook in the preheated oven for 45 minutes. Remove the garlic and let cool. When cool enough to handle, squeeze the soft, baked garlic directly into the bowl of a food processor or blender and discard the skin. Add the remaining ingredients and process until smooth. Transfer to a serving dish and cover until ready to serve.

beet and caraway dip

3 medium beets, uncooked
1 tablespoon prepared horseradish sauce
½ cup sour cream
1 teaspoon caraway seeds
sea salt and white pepper

Serves 6–8

Put the beet in a large saucepan and cover with cold water. Bring to a boil and let boil for about 45–50 minutes, topping up the water from time to time as necessary. They are ready when a skewer goes through them with little resistance. Drain and let cool. When cool enough to handle, peel and discard the skins. Roughly chop and put in a food processor or blender with the other ingredients and process until smooth. Transfer to a serving dish and cover until ready to serve.

spiced carrot dip

1 cup vegetable stock
4 medium carrots, chopped
2 tablespoons light olive oil
1 small red onion, chopped
2 garlic cloves, chopped
1 large red chile, chopped
1 teaspoon fenugreek seeds
1 teaspoon ground cumin
sea salt and white pepper

Serves 6–8

Put the stock in a saucepan and add the carrots, oil, onion and garlic. Bring to a boil, then reduce the heat to low and simmer for 15–20 minutes, until almost all the liquid has evaporated and the carrots are soft. Add the chile, fenugreek, and cumin and stir-fry for 2–3 minutes. Transfer the mixture to a food processor or blender and whizz until blended but still with a rough texture. Season to taste, transfer to a serving dish and cover until ready to serve.

spelt toasts

¾ cup spelt
1 tablespoon dried yeast
2 cups spelt flour
½ teaspoon sea salt
all-purpose flour, for dusting

Makes about 40 toasts

Put the spelt in a strainer and rinse under cold running water. Put it in a saucepan with 4 cups water and bring to a boil. Reduce the heat to low, cover with a lid and cook for 45 minutes. Remove the lid and boil rapidly until almost all the liquid has evaporated. Meanwhile, put the yeast in a small bowl with ½ cup warm water, stir, cover, and let rest in a warm place until the mixture is frothy. While it is still warm, put the spelt in a bowl with the spelt flour, salt, 1 cup tepid water, and the yeast and stir to bring the mixture together to form a sticky dough. Put the dough on a lightly floured counter and gently knead for 1 minute. Carefully transfer the dough to a lightly oiled bowl, cover with a kitchen towel and let rise in a warm place for about 1–1¼ hours, until it has risen and doubled in size.

Preheat the oven to 400°F. Tip the dough out onto a lightly oiled baking sheet and, using floured hands, form the dough into a loaf about 8 x 4 inches, tapering at the ends. Bake the bread in the preheated oven for 40 minutes. Carefully slide the loaf off the baking sheet and directly onto the oven shelf, then bake for a further 5 minutes. Remove from the oven and let cool. To serve, slice into ¼-inch wide pieces and toast under a hot broiler until golden and crispy on both sides.

crispy onion rings with Parmesan aioli

These are a good thing to cook at the same time as the croquettes, especially if, like me, you don't cook fried food often. You don't have to be too fussy and cook one ring at a time—they taste just as delicious cooked in clumps. Enjoy them warm with the aioli as a dip.

2 red onions, thinly sliced

2 white onions, thinly sliced

1 cup buttermilk (or 1 cup whole milk combined with 1 tablespoon lemon juice)

6 tablespoons chickpea flour

6 tablespoons cornstarch

1 teaspoon sea salt

2 eggs

2 cups vegetable oil

Parmesan aioli:

2 egg yolks

2 garlic cloves, crushed

2 teaspoons freshly squeezed lemon juice

¾ cup light olive oil

¼ cup finely grated Parmesan cheese

sea salt and white pepper

Serves 4

To make the aioli, put the egg yolks, garlic, and lemon juice in a small bowl and whisk until just combined. Whisk constantly as you add the oil, very slowly at first but building up to a steady stream. Stir in the Parmesan and season with salt and pepper. Set aside.

Put the onion slices in a large bowl and gently toss to separate the rings. Add the buttermilk and stir. Set aside for 1 hour. Put the chickpea flour, cornstarch, and salt in a bowl. Make a small well in the center. Use a slotted spoon to remove the onions from the buttermilk (reserving the buttermilk) and transfer them to a colander to drain off any excess liquid. Put ½ cup of the reserved buttermilk in a bowl and beat in the eggs until just combined. Pour this mixture into the flour mixture and beat well with a wooden spoon to form a smooth, thick batter.

Put the oil in a skillet set over medium/high heat. Toss a handful of onion rings into the batter and lift them out with a slotted spoon (letting any excess batter drip back into the bowl). Put them in the skillet. Cook for about 1 minute, or until golden. Remove from the oil with a slotted spoon and drain on paper towels. Repeat with the remaining onion rings. Serve warm with the Parmesan aioli.

potato and parsnip croquettes

Some form of fried potato croquette turns up in almost all styles of cuisine including German, Dutch, Spanish, and the delicious alloo ki tiki from India. I guess they must be so popular because of the harmonious pairing of potatoes, salt, and hot oil. I like to use a floury potato for these croquettes, such as Idaho, as it fluffs up nicely when boiled and mashed. The parsnip adds an interesting flavor dimension, as it is a little bitter and sweet at the same time.

1 lb. potatoes, peeled and quartered

1 parsnip, peeled and quartered

3 tablespoons butter

2 tablespoons finely chopped parsley

2 eggs

1 cup dry breadcrumbs from a day-old loaf of bread

2 tablespoons all-purpose flour, for dusting

vegetable oil, for shallow-frying

sea salt and freshly ground black pepper

sweet German mustard, to serve

Makes 18 croquettes

Put the potatoes and parsnip in a large saucepan and cover with boiling water. Set over high heat and boil for 12–15 minutes until tender. Drain and return to the warm pan. Add 2 tablespoons of the butter and mash well until the mixture is lump-free. Stir in the parsley and season well with salt and pepper. Cover and refrigerate until the mixture is completely chilled.

Break the eggs into a bowl and beat well to combine. Put the breadcrumbs in a separate bowl. Lightly flour your hands and counter. Take 1 heaped tablespoon of mixture and form it into a small sausage, tapping the ends on the floured counter so that they are flattened rather than tapered. Dip the croquette in the beaten egg, then roll it in the crumbs until coated. Put on a sheet or baking sheet lined with waxed paper. Repeat until all of the potato mixture has been used and refrigerate until ready to cook.

Put the remaining 1 tablespoon butter in a skillet and pour in sufficient oil to come halfway up the sides of the pan. Heat the skillet over medium heat until the butter begins to sizzle. To test if the oil is hot enough, sprinkle a few crumbs into it—they should sizzle on contact. Cook the croquettes in batches for 2–3 minutes, turning often, until golden and crisp all over. Remove from the oil using a slotted spoon and drain on paper towels to remove excess oil. Serve warm with the mustard on the side.

When was the last time you stirred some freshly made pesto into a big bowl of hot spaghetti? It's an aromatic and heady experience. Food manufacturers like us to believe that pesto keeps in a jar or plastic tub in the fridge, but I couldn't disagree more. It soon oxidizes, turning bitter, brown and oily, and quickly becomes a lesser version of its glorious former self. This vibrant pesto made with handfuls of garden-fresh basil and parsley will knock your socks off and surpass anything you can buy at a store.

crispy oven wedges with homemade pesto sauce

2 large, floury potatoes (such as Idaho), each cut into 8–10 wedges
2 tablespoons light olive oil

pesto sauce:
2 handfuls of fresh basil leaves
1 handful of fresh flat-leaf parsley leaves
1 garlic clove, chopped
1 tablespoon freshly squeezed lemon juice
⅓ cup pine nuts, lightly toasted
¼ cup light olive oil
½ cup finely grated Parmesan cheese

Serves 4

To make the pesto, put the basil, parsley, garlic, lemon juice, and pine nuts in a food processor and process until finely chopped. With the motor of the food processor running, add the oil in a steady stream until it is all incorporated, then transfer the mixture to a bowl and stir in the Parmesan. Cover and set aside until you are ready to serve.

Bring a large saucepan of water to a boil and add the potatoes. Boil them for 5 minutes, then drain and let cool completely.

Preheat the oven to 425°F. Drizzle the oil onto a large, shallow roasting pan and put in the oven for 5 minutes to heat up. Arrange the potatoes on the pan in a single layer and bake in the preheated oven for about 8 minutes, until they are golden on the underside. Turn them over and cook for another 8 minutes, until crisp and golden all over.

Transfer the hot wedges to a plate and serve with the pesto on the side to use as a dip.

These fun little Chinese dumplings are called potstickers because of the technique of first pan-frying their bottoms until they are crisp and golden, then pouring over stock (or water), quickly covering, and letting them steam in the resulting hot vapor. I have used gow gee wrappers here, which are available from Chinese markets. If you can't find them, you can use wonton wrappers.

vegetable potstickers with orange dipping sauce

3 cups finely shredded red cabbage

1 teaspoon sea salt flakes

2 tablespoons vegetable oil, plus about ¼ cup for shallow-frying

1 tablespoon finely grated fresh ginger

4 garlic cloves, finely chopped

1 small carrot, grated

1 tablespoon light soy sauce

18 gow gee wrappers

½ cup vegetable stock

4 scallions, thinly sliced

1 handful of roughly chopped fresh cilantro

freshly ground black pepper

orange dipping sauce:

¼ cup light soy sauce

¼ cup rice vinegar

¼ cup freshly squeezed orange juice

Makes 18 small dumplings

To make the dipping sauce, put all of the ingredients in a bowl and whisk to combine. Cover and set aside until ready to serve.

Put the cabbage in a bowl and sprinkle over the sea salt. Cover and let sit for 30 minutes, stirring a few times. Put the cabbage in a colander and squeeze out as much liquid as possible. Tip it onto a chopping board and finely chop. Transfer to a bowl and set aside.

Put the 2 tablespoons oil in a non-stick skillet or wok and set over high heat. Add the ginger and garlic and stir-fry for just a few seconds to soften the ingredients and flavor the oil. Add the cabbage and carrot and stir-fry for 1 minute. Add the soy sauce and season with black pepper. Transfer to a bowl and let cool.

Put 2 teaspoons of the mixture in the center of a gow gee wrapper. Brush around the edges with a little water and bring the two sides together to form a half-moon shape, snugly enclosing the filling. Press the edges firmly and crimp or pleat around the edges to seal. Gently tap the dumplings on their base so that they get a flattened bottom. Put the dumplings on a baking sheet lined with parchment paper, cover and refrigerate until you are ready to cook them.

Cook the potstickers in 2 batches. Put half of the oil for shallow-frying in a cast-iron skillet and set over medium heat. Add the first batch of potstickers to the pan and cook for 2–3 minutes until the bottoms sizzle in the oil and turn crisp and golden. Shake the pan while they are cooking so that they don't stick. Carefully add half of the stock, standing well back from the pan, as it will splutter. Quickly cover with a lid and let cook for 2–3 minutes, until the dumplings are steamed and the filling is cooked through. Cook the second batch in the same way. Sprinkle with cilantro and scallions and serve warm with the orange dipping sauce on the side.

Modern Spanish tapas bars are very popular just now. I hope it's not just a passing trend and that they are here to stay, as tapas dishes are casual, shared food at its very best. Mushrooms really are nature's cups just waiting to be filled. Look for ones that will be two to three small mouthfuls when cooked—big cremini mushrooms or smaller portobellos are both ideal. These are very rich, so a crisp fennel salad is the perfect accompaniment.

baked mushrooms with Manchego béchamel

2 teaspoons butter

2 teaspoons all-purpose flour

½ cup whole milk

½ cup finely grated Manchego cheese

12 wide, flat mushrooms

¼ teaspoon smoked Spanish paprika (pimentón)

fennel salad:

1 small fennel bulb

1 handful of fresh flat-leaf parsley leaves

2 teaspoons olive oil

2 teaspoons freshly squeezed lemon juice

sea salt and freshly ground black pepper

Serves 4–6

Put the butter in a small saucepan and cook over high heat until it is melted and sizzling. Before the butter burns, add the flour and stir quickly to form a thick paste. Remove from the heat and add a little of the milk, stirring constantly until thick and smooth. Return the pan to medium heat and add the remaining milk, whisking constantly until all the milk is incorporated and the mixture is smooth and thick. Remove from the heat and let cool.

Preheat the oven to 425°F. Remove the stalks from the mushrooms and sit the mushrooms in a small baking dish, gill-side up. Spoon the sauce into the caps and sprinkle the paprika over the top. Cook in the preheated oven for 20 minutes, until the mushrooms are soft and the sauce is golden and bubbling.

While the mushrooms are cooking, slice the fennel bulb as thinly as possible, chop the fronds and put in a bowl with the parsley, oil, and lemon juice. Toss to combine, season to taste, and serve with the warm mushrooms.

zucchini and mint fritters with spicy tomato jam

This is a quick, no-fuss tomato jam. Keep your eye on the chiles—they can be eye-wateringly hot and turn your jam into something only a few die-hards would enjoy. It's best to remove all the seeds initially, then take it from there. This rich-colored jam is also delicious served with the Spelt Toasts on page 18 and a big chunk of sharp cheddar.

2 zucchini, grated

2 oz. feta cheese, crumbled

10–12 fresh mint leaves, finely shredded

2 egg whites

1 tablespoon cornstarch

3 tablespoons olive oil

spicy tomato jam:

4 ripe tomatoes, halved

1 large red chile, seeded and thinly sliced

1 tablespoon olive oil

1 garlic clove, crushed

1 teaspoon white sugar

Makes 12 fritters

To make the jam, preheat the oven to 425°F. Line a baking sheet with parchment paper. Put the tomatoes in a bowl with the chile and oil and toss to coat. Arrange them cut-side up on the prepared sheet and cook in the preheated oven for 30 minutes, until just starting to collapse and soften. Transfer them to the bowl of a food processor, add the garlic and sugar and process until smooth. Transfer the mixture to a saucepan and cook over high heat until it reaches a boil. Continue to boil for about 10 minutes until it has reduced in volume by half. Spoon into a bowl and let cool.

Put the zucchini, feta, and mint in a bowl and stir to combine. In a separate, grease-free bowl, whisk the egg whites until they are white and frothy. Add the cornstarch and whisk until the cornstarch has dissolved. Tip the zucchini mixture into the egg whites and gently fold in until combined.

Heat the oil in a non-stick skillet over high heat. Cook the fritters in 2 batches. Spoon 1 heaped tablespoon of the mixture into the skillet and press down lightly to form a flat fritter. Repeat to create 5 more fritters. Fry for 2 minutes on each side until a dark, golden brown. Carefully lift the cooked fritters onto paper towels to drain any excess oil. Repeat this process to make a second batch of 6 fritters. Serve hot with the spicy tomato jam.

tempura of mixed veggies with citrus dipping sauce

Like origami, tempura is often perceived as an art form not to be attempted without a manual. This couldn't be further from the truth. Just follow a few simple rules. Use crisp vegetables without too high a water content (I tried this with endive and lettuce with disappointing results). Ice water is essential, as it ensures the batter is light and lacy. Don't overbeat the batter—a few quick stirs with a chopstick is all that is required and any lumps will just add texture to the cooked batter.

8 asparagus spears, ends trimmed

1 yellow bell pepper, cut into ¼-inch strips

1 red bell pepper, cut into ¼-inch strips

2 cups vegetable oil

6 tablespoons cornstarch

1 cup all-purpose flour

¼ teaspoon baking powder

½ teaspoon salt

1⅓ cups ml ice water

citrus dipping sauce:

¼ cup Japanese soy sauce

1 tablespoon freshly squeezed lemon juice

1 tablespoon freshly squeezed lime juice

1 tablespoon freshly squeezed orange juice

Serves 4

To make the citrus dipping sauce, put all of the ingredients in a small bowl and whisk to combine. Set aside until ready to serve.

Put the prepared vegetables on a plate near to your stove top. Put the oil in a skillet and set over medium/high heat. Combine the cornstarch, all-purpose flour, baking powder, and salt in a bowl. Put the ice water in another chilled bowl. Working quickly, add the flour mixture to the cold water, stirring for just a few seconds with a chopstick or a knife, leaving the mixture lumpy-looking.

Cook the tempura in batches. Add a small handful of vegetables to the batter, letting any excess batter drip back into the bowl. Cook for 2–3 minutes, turning often with tongs so that the batter cooks evenly all over and is lightly golden and lacy looking. Put the tempura on some paper towels for a minute to absorb any excess oil. Reheat the oil and repeat with the remaining vegetables and batter. Serve warm with the citrus dipping sauce on the side.

See photograph on page 30.

cauliflower and caperberries on halloumi

Cauliflower is transformed when cooked in a generous amount of olive oil with classic Middle Eastern flavorings such as cumin, tahini, and lemon juice. I look for any excuse to include halloumi cheese in a recipe, but the cauliflower mixture here could also be served as a topping on crisply toasted sourdough bread. If you enjoy spicy foods, try a light sprinkle of dried hot pepper flakes for a piquant appetizer. If you like cauliflower, you could also try the warm Cauliflower and Swiss Chard Salad on page 53.

3 tablespoons olive oil

10 oz. cauliflower, broken into small florets

2 garlic cloves, chopped

⅓ cup caperberries, large ones halved

⅔ cup green olives, pitted and sliced

3 tablespoons chopped fresh flat-leaf parsley

1 tablespoon freshly squeezed lemon juice

2 teaspoons light olive oil

10 oz. halloumi cheese, cut into ¼-inch thick slices

sea salt and freshly ground black pepper

Serves 4–6

Heat the olive oil in a skillet and cook the cauliflower florets for 8–10 minutes over high heat, stirring often until they brown evenly and start to crisp up. Add the garlic, caperberries, olives, parsley, and lemon juice and cook for 2 minutes, stirring constantly. Season to taste and leave in the skillet to keep warm.

Heat the light olive oil in a non-stick skillet set over high heat. Cook the halloumi slices for 1 minute on each side, until golden brown. Transfer the halloumi to serving plates and spoon the warm cauliflower mixture over each one. Serve immediately.

See photograph on page 31.

spicy tomato, black bean, and feta dip with organic tortilla chips

The fresh flavors in this Tex-Mex-style dip seem to have a natural affinity with tortilla chips. This is a twist on the popular chili con queso, usually made with cheddar or mozzarella. I find the flavor of cheddar too overpowering and the texture a little greasy with the mildly spiced flavors here, so I opt for Greek feta instead. It doesn't entirely melt, but softens and adds a salty bite to the dip, which enhances the sweetness of the tomatoes and bell pepper. If you are in a hurry, you can easily substitute the dried beans with canned red kidney beans.

½ cup dried black beans

1 tablespoon olive oil

1 small red bell pepper, thinly sliced

1 red onion, thinly sliced

1 teaspoon ground cumin

2 garlic cloves, finely chopped

2 small red chiles, finely chopped

3 tomatoes, chopped

1 tablespoon red wine vinegar

1 cup passata or tomato purée

6 oz. feta cheese, crumbled

organic tortilla chips, to serve

Serves 4

Soak the black beans in cold water overnight. Drain and rinse well. Put them in a large saucepan with plenty of water and bring to a boil. Cook for 25–30 minutes, until soft to the bite. Drain well and set aside.

Heat the oil in a saucepan set over high heat and add the red bell pepper and onion. Reduce the heat to low, cover, and cook for about 8 minutes. Add the cumin, garlic, and chiles and cook for a further 2 minutes. Add the beans, tomatoes, vinegar, and passata and bring to a boil. Reduce the heat and simmer rapidly for about 10 minutes, until almost all the liquid has evaporated and the tomatoes start to look mushy. Transfer to a flame-proof dish and sprinkle the crumbled feta over the top. Cook under a preheated high broiler until the cheese is soft and just starting to brown. Serve hot with tortilla chips on the side for dipping.

This is simple tapas-style food for sharing at its best. The tortilla may not look that substantial, but thanks to the creamy Taleggio cheese, it packs a super-rich taste punch and is more than enough for four people to enjoy as an appetizer or snack. Keep your eyes peeled for nice little new potatoes when you are out shopping. Sometimes you will only be able to find boiling potatoes that are the size of a golf ball, but at other times you'll see deliciously nutty little potatoes (the size of a shelled walnut) like the ones I've used here. The red bell pepper tapenade is a versatile recipe to have in your repertoire. It can be tossed through pasta, spooned over grilled vegetables, and stirred into soup. Try it with the Summer Sweetcorn Soup on page 66.

Taleggio and potato tortilla with red pepper tapenade

10–12 small, new, boiling potatoes, thickly sliced

1 small red onion, roughly chopped

1 tablespoon olive oil

1 cup vegetable stock

1 handful of fresh flat-leaf parsley, chopped

4 oz. Taleggio cheese, chopped or torn into large chunks

2 eggs, lightly beaten

red pepper tapenade:

1 large red bell pepper

1 garlic clove, chopped

⅓ cup pine nuts, lightly toasted

2 tablespoons olive oil

½ cup finely grated Parmesan cheese

Serves 4

To make the tapenade, preheat the oven to 425°F. Put a baking sheet in the oven for a few minutes to heat. Put the red bell pepper on the sheet and cook it in the preheated oven for about 15 minutes, turning often until the skin is starting to blacken and puff up. Transfer it to a clean plastic bag and let cool. When the bell pepper is cool enough to handle, peel off the skin, roughly tear or chop the flesh, and put it in a food processor. Add the garlic, pine nuts, and oil and process until smooth. Spoon into a bowl, add the Parmesan and stir well to combine.

Put the potatoes, onion, and oil in a skillet set over high heat and cook for 1 minute. Add the stock and cook for 10 minutes, until the stock has evaporated and the vegetables start to sizzle in the skillet. Stir through the parsley and put the pieces of cheese among the potatoes. Pour the eggs into the pan and cook for 2–3 minutes until they start to puff up around the edges. Give the skillet a couple of firm shakes—this will make it easier to get the cooked tortilla out. Meanwhile, preheat the broiler to high. Put the skillet under the hot broiler and cook the tortilla for 1–2 minutes, until the top is golden but still wobbly in the center. Use a spatula to smear some of the tapenade onto the base of a serving plate and carefully slide the tortilla onto the plate. Cut into 4 slices and eat direct from the plate with extra tapenade on the side for spooning.

summer grazing platter

The soda bread was really the inspiration for the other little dishes here. This is a no-fuss, dead-easy bread to make and it also freezes and toasts well. I have enjoyed this with cheese and home-made quince paste in cooler months. But here we have the best of summer's bounty—tasty little plates to graze on during a summer's afternoon. Serve with a generous slice of sharp cheddar.

pumpkin and caraway seed soda bread

10½ oz. pie pumpkin or butternut squash, peeled, seeded, and cut into chunks
1 tablespoon molasses
1 cup self-rising whole-wheat flour
1 cup fine semolina
1 tablespoon caraway seeds
1 teaspoon salt
½ cup soda water

Makes 1 medium loaf

Preheat the oven to 400°F. Cook the pumpkin in a saucepan of boiling water for 10 minutes until soft when pierced with a skewer. Drain and return to the warm pan. Add the molasses and mash to a chunky paste. Put the flours in a bowl with the caraway seeds and salt and use a whisk to stir to combine. Form a well in the center and add the pumpkin while it is still warm. Use a large spoon to stir for 1 minute, then gradually stir through the soda water until you have a chunky mix that is just combined. Do not overmix. Working quickly, lightly flour a counter, turn the dough out and use your hands to form it into an oval. Put the dough on a baking sheet dusted with a little fine semolina and use a sharp knife to make 3–4 shallow diagonal slices across the top of the loaf. Bake in the preheated oven for 30 minutes. Open the door to the oven, leaving the oven on and cook for a further 10 minutes. This will give the bread a nice dry crust. Remove from the oven and let cool on a wire rack.

corn relish

1 tablespoon olive oil
kernels from 2 ears of corn, about 1½ cups
1 small red bell pepper, thinly sliced
1 small red onion, thinly sliced
1 garlic clove, finely chopped
1 tablespoon brown sugar
½ cup vegetable stock
2 teaspoons hot English mustard
½ cup cider vinegar
1 teaspoon cornstarch

Serves 4–6

Heat the oil in a skillet set over high heat and add the corn kernels, red bell pepper, and onion. Cook for 5 minutes, stirring constantly. Add the garlic and cook, stirring, for 1 minute. Stir in the sugar, add the stock and bring to a boil. Reduce the heat and let simmer for about 10 minutes, until almost all the liquid has evaporated.

Put the mustard, vinegar, and cornstarch in a small bowl and mix well. Add this mixture to the corn and cook over high heat for 1 minute, until the liquid thickens and coats the corn. Remove from the heat and let cool before serving.

pickled eggplant

1 cup white wine vinegar
1 eggplant, chopped
1 large red chile, sliced
1 garlic clove, sliced
½ teaspoon caraway seeds
3 tablespoons olive oil

Makes 1½ cups

Put the vinegar in a small saucepan with 2 cups water and bring to a boil. Add the eggplant, cover with a lid, and turn off the heat. Let the eggplant sit in the liquid for about 20 minutes. Drain well and let the eggplant cool completely. Put the eggplant in a bowl with the chile, garlic, caraway seeds, and oil. Cover and refrigerate for 1 day before eating.

slow-roasted tomatoes

8 ripe Italian tomatoes, such as Roma, halved
1 tablespoon olive oil
½ teaspoon sea salt
½ teaspoon white sugar
1 teaspoon ground cumin

Serves 4–6

Preheat the oven to 350°F. Put the tomatoes in a bowl with the other ingredients and toss to coat in the oil. Put the tomatoes, cut-side up, on a baking sheet and roast in the preheated oven for 1 hour, until they are starting to blacken around the edges. Serve warm.

midweek
meals

This gorgeous-looking and delicious rice dish is inspired by the salade Niçoise, the popular plate from southern France. This version doesn't include the tuna and anchovies, but you can add these if you like. What it does have is generous handfuls of market-fresh herbs and the key flavors of summer-ripe tomatoes, black olives, green beans and hard-boiled eggs.

Niçoise-style brown rice salad with fresh herbs

4 eggs

7 oz. baby green beans

12 oz. short-grain brown rice

¼ cup olive oil

1 garlic clove, crushed

2 tablespoons freshly squeezed lemon juice

7 oz. cherry tomatoes, halved

3 oz. black olives, pitted and halved

1 small of bunch fresh chives, finely snipped

1 large handful of fresh parsley, chopped

1 large handful of fresh basil leaves

1 large handful of fresh mint leaves

1 small handful of fresh tarragon leaves

sea salt and freshly ground black pepper

Serves 4

Put the eggs in a small saucepan and cover with cold water. Set over high heat and bring to a boil. Cook for 3 minutes, then rinse under cold water. When cool enough to handle, peel and halve them then set aside.

Cook the beans in boiling water for 1 minute. Drain and put in a bowl of cold water. Put the rice in a strainer and rinse well under cold running water. Transfer the rice to a large saucepan and add sufficient just-boiled water. Set the pan over high heat, return the water to a boil and cook the rice for 10–12 minutes until it is tender but retains some "bite". Tip the rice into a strainer, rinse under cold running water, and drain well. Put the rice and drained beans in a large bowl and add the oil, garlic, and lemon juice. Stir until the rice is coated in the oil. Add the tomatoes, olives, and herbs, toss to combine and season to taste with salt and pepper. Arrange the egg halves on top to serve.

old-fashioned garden salad with garlic toasts

We all have childhood memories of food. I recall that in summer (and this is well and truly before the days of mass-produced salad dressings), a bowl of salad cream would sit on the table ready to be spooned over a simple salad. To my young taste buds, the flavors were at first challenging and then addictive; tangy, creamy, and sweet all at once. I really wanted to capture the spirit of this dressing and my research led me to the recipes of Constance Spry, famous for coronation chicken and, as I discovered, salad cream. I have tweaked the ingredients, making them more modern, but the fresh, summer garden produce is the same and the crisp garlic toasts add a contemporary crunch.

6 thin slices of Italian bread, such as ciabatta
3–4 garlic cloves
1 baby romaine lettuce
1 small round butterhead lettuce
1 handful of curly endive or escarole
3 ripe tomatoes
1 bunch of scallions
7 oz. sharp cheddar, thinly sliced
2 hard-boiled eggs, quartered
olive oil, for brushing or drizzling

salad cream:
1 teaspoon sea salt flakes
1 teaspoon superfine sugar
1 tablespoon mild mustard, such as Dijon
1 tablespoon white wine vinegar
¼ cup olive oil
6 tablespoons whole milk

Serves 4

To make the salad cream, put the salt, sugar, mustard, vinegar, and oil in a bowl and whisk to dissolve the salt and sugar. Begin to add the milk, very slowly at first and whisking the whole time. Continue to add all of the milk until you have a dressing the consistency of a thin custard.

Brush or drizzle a little oil over each side of the bread slices. Lightly toast the bread until golden on both sides and rub the garlic cloves over the toast. Allow the toast to cool and crisp up.

Combine the salad ingredients in a large bowl. Roughly break up the pieces of toast and add to the salad with some of the salad cream then gently toss to combine. Serve immediately.

salad of winter fruit with blue cheese and spinach

I am so happy we have finally moved on from the need to have the perfect red or green apple displayed in the supermarket—row upon row of them, all polished to a high shine and flawless. That said, the vast number of organically grown apple and pear varieties at your local farmers' market might be a little overwhelming! If you are unsure, my tip is to ask your market supplier a few simple questions such as what varieties are good for cooking, for munching on or, as here, slicing directly into a salad bowl with a few other great ingredients. I have chosen firm, woody-looking fruit for this recipe, just how it ought to look when you pick it straight from the tree.

2 apples, cored and cut into thin wedges
2 firm pears, cored and cut into thin wedges
1 small head of radicchio, leaves separated
2 large handfuls of fresh spinach leaves
7 oz. firm blue cheese, crumbled

tarragon vinaigrette:
3 tablespoons light olive oil
1 tablespoon tarragon vinegar
¼ teaspoon freshly cracked white pepper
sea salt

Serves 4

Combine the apples, pears, radicchio, spinach, and blue cheese in a large salad bowl and toss gently to combine. Whisk the oil, vinegar, and pepper in a small bowl and season with a little sea salt. Pour the dressing over the salad, toss well and serve immediately.

See photograph on page 45.

garlic and chile rice soup with wilted greens

This is a substantial soup—really more of a light stew. Boiled rice soups are popular in many Asian countries, especially China where they are called congees. They are often eaten for breakfast, but are an acquired taste as the rice is boiled until it breaks down to form a rather viscous white "porridge". The greens can be collards or the fresh, young outer leaves of brassicas such as cabbage. They work very nicely with the simple Asian flavors here.

1 tablespoon vegetable oil
2 teaspoons sesame oil
2 garlic cloves, chopped
4 scallions, finely chopped
2 teaspoons finely grated fresh ginger
1 small red chile, seeded and thinly sliced
½ cup long-grain white rice
6 cups vegetable stock
1 tablespoon soy sauce or Thai fish sauce
1 bunch of collard green, roughly shredded
1 small bunch of fresh cilantro, chopped
white pepper

Serves 2

Put the oils in a saucepan and set over high heat. Add the garlic and scallions and cook until the garlic is turning golden and just starting to burn. This will give the soup a lovely, nutty garlic flavor. Add the ginger, chile, and rice to the pan and stir-fry in the garlic-infused oil for 1 minute. Add the stock and soy sauce and bring to a boil.

Cover with a lid and cook over low heat for 30 minutes, until the rice is soft and the soup has thickened. Add the collard greens and cook for 5 minutes, until they turn emerald green and are tender. Ladle the soup into warmed serving bowls, sprinkle the cilantro over the top and season to taste with pepper.

oven-baked zucchini and tomato risotto

This is a super-speedy dish. As with any recipe for a baked risotto, you are not going to get the creamy texture of one cooked by the more conventional method. That said, this recipe more than makes up for it in other ways—take simple, fresh ingredients, a few quick stirs and dinner is ready to serve.

3 cups vegetable stock
2 tablespoons olive oil
1 onion, chopped
1 garlic clove, chopped
1½ cups short-grain white rice
2 tablespoons fresh rosemary needles
2 zucchini, roughly chopped
2 tomatoes, chopped
3 tablespoons butter
½ cup finely grated Parmesan cheese

Serves 4

Preheat the oven to 400°C. Put the stock in a large saucepan and set over low heat. Put the oil in a flameproof, lidded casserole dish and set over low heat. Add the onion and garlic and sauté gently for 2–3 minutes until the onion has softened. Add the rice and the rosemary and cook for a further minute before adding the zucchini. Stir for 1 minute, or until the rice becomes opaque, then add the tomatoes. Pour the hot stock into the casserole and stir well to remove any stuck-on bits and to combine all the ingredients. As soon as the liquid starts to simmer, cover with the lid and cook in the preheated oven for 30 minutes.

Stir through the butter and half of the Parmesan, then sprinkle the remaining Parmesan on top to serve.

See photograph on page 48.

linguine with heirloom tomatoes, red endive, and black olives

This pasta recipe involves the Italian technique of gently blanching the garlic in warm oil so that it softens and imparts its flavor without dominating the other fresh ingredients. When it comes to tomatoes, we are spoilt for choice during the summer months, so I like to use a number of interesting varieties, heirloom if possible, and mix up the colors. The bitter red endive leaves offset the fruity sweetness of the tomatoes.

¼ cup olive oil
4 garlic cloves, chopped
6 medium tomatoes, roughly chopped
1 red Belgian endive, leaves torn
1 handful of small black olives
14 oz. linguine
½ cup finely grated Parmesan cheese
sea salt and freshly ground black pepper

Serves 4

Heat the oil in a large skillet, add the garlic and cook over medium heat for a couple of minutes, to soften, but don't let it burn. Add the tomatoes to the pan and cook for 2–3 minutes so that they are just soft and starting to break up. Remove from the heat, stir through the endive leaves and olives and season with salt and pepper. Set aside while cooking the pasta.

Cook the pasta according to the package instructions. Drain well and put in a large bowl. Add the tomato sauce and half of the Parmesan and toss to combine. Serve with extra Parmesan on top.

See photograph on page 49.

braised fennel with polenta

Always buy fennel with the feathery leaves intact, as these can be added to the final stages of a dish or used as a garnish. While smaller, tender bulbs can be eaten raw, the larger, tougher ones are perfect when braised, as here.

2 large fennel bulbs
¼ cup light olive oil
1 onion, chopped
2 garlic cloves, chopped
1 small red chile, chopped
1 handful of fresh flat-leaf parsley leaves, roughly chopped
2 tablespoons freshly squeezed lemon juice
2 tablespoons sweet white wine
2 cups vegetable stock
1 handful of small black olives
grated Pecorino cheese, to serve

creamy polenta:
2 cups whole milk
4 cups vegetable stock
1¼ cups instant polenta
3 tablespoons butter
1 cup finely grated Pecorino Romano cheese

Serves 4

Cut about ¼ inch from the gnarly stem on the bottom of the fennel bulbs. Cut off the fronds, chop finely, and reserve. Cut off and discard all but about ½ inch from the dark green stems. Thinly slice the remaining white fennel bulb lengthwise. Put the oil in a heavy-based saucepan and set over high heat. Add the onions, garlic, and chiles and cook for 2–3 minutes until softened. Add the parsley and fennel bulb and fronds and cook for 2–3 minutes, stirring often so that the fennel becomes coated in the oil. Add the lemon juice, wine, and stock and bring to a boil. Cover with a lid and turn the heat down to a low simmer for 20 minutes, stirring occasionally. Add the olives, remove the lid and boil rapidly until there is only a little liquid left and the fennel is very soft.

Meanwhile, to make the polenta, put the milk and stock in a saucepan and bring to a gentle simmer over medium heat. Slowly pour in the polenta in a steady stream and beat with a balloon whisk until smooth. Reduce the heat to low and continue to beat for 4–5 minutes. When the mixture thickens, discard the whisk and use a wooden spoon. Add the butter and cheese and stir until melted into the polenta. Spoon some polenta onto serving plates, top with the braised fennel and sprinkle with grated Pecorino to serve.

spaghetti with broccoli, walnuts, and ricotta

The light texture and creamy flavor of ricotta cheese makes the perfect backdrop to walnuts and broccoli in this deliciously simple and quick pasta dish.

⅔ cup walnut halves
1 head of broccoli, about 1 lb.
3 tablespoons light olive oil
3 garlic cloves, thinly sliced
1 handful of fresh flat-leaf parsley, chopped
finely grated zest and freshly squeezed juice of 1 unwaxed lemon
7 oz. fresh ricotta cheese
14 oz. spaghetti
sea salt and freshly ground black pepper

Serves 4

Preheat the oven to 350°F. Spread the walnuts out on a baking sheet and roast in the preheated oven for about 8 minutes, shaking the sheet occasionally, until they start to brown.

To prepare the broccoli, trim off the gnarly part, about 1 inch from the stem end, and discard. Thinly slice the stem until you reach the point where it starts to branch into florets. Slice off the individual florets. Heat the oil in a skillet, add the stems, and cook for about 2–3 minutes, turning often, then add the florets and cook for about 5 minutes, until the broccoli has softened. Add the garlic, parsley, lemon zest, and walnuts and cook for 5 minutes, stirring often. Reduce the heat to medium and stir through the ricotta and lemon juice. Season to taste with salt and pepper and leave in the skillet to keep warm.

Cook the spaghetti according to the package instructions. Drain well and return it to the warm pan with the sauce. Stir gently to combine and serve immediately.

cauliflower and Swiss chard salad

The distinctive thick leaves that seem to hug the head of a cauliflower are actually protecting the white "flower" from the sun. In doing so, they deprive it of what it needs to turn green, and that's essentially the difference between the cauliflower and its close relative broccoli. I'm a huge fan of cauliflower, but it is so often overlooked in favor of other brassicas, such as broccoli, that are quicker to cook. I like its intense flavor and use it often in creamy soups and curries or, as I have done here, in a light and spicy Middle Eastern-style salad.

¼ cup light olive oil
1 small head of cauliflower, separated into large florets
1 teaspoon ground cumin
6 large Swiss chard leaves, chopped into 1-inch wide strips
1 red onion, cut into wedges
2 garlic cloves, chopped
14-oz can chickpeas, rinsed and drained
¼ cup tahini (sesame seed paste)
2 tablespoons freshly squeezed lemon juice
¼ teaspoon freshly cracked white pepper
sea salt

Serves 4

Put the oil in a skillet set over high heat, add the cauliflower florets and cook for 8–10 minutes, turning often, until they are a dark, golden brown. Add the cumin and cook, stirring, for 1 minute. Add the Swiss chard, onion, and garlic to the skillet and cook for a further 2–3 minutes. Add the chickpeas and stir. Season to taste with salt.

Combine the tahini, lemon juice, and pepper in a small bowl and add a little salt to taste. Whisk to combine. Transfer the vegetables to a bowl and drizzle the dressing over the top to serve.

See photograph on page 54.

broccoli, shiitake, and tofu omelet

This is an omelette with a distinctly Asian feel with creamy cubes of tofu replacing the more traditional cheese. This is perfect for a light, midweek supper, but I've occasionally enjoyed it as a weekend brunch. As a variation, you can replace the broccoli with young, tender peas and add a sprinkling of fresh cilantro.

1 tablespoon light olive oil
2 shallots, sliced
1 bunch of tenderstem broccoli (broccolini), chopped into small pieces
7 oz. shiitake mushrooms
1 cup baby spinach leaves
2 teaspoons light soy sauce
10 oz. firm tofu, cubed
8 eggs, lightly beaten
ground white pepper
oyster sauce, to serve (optional)

Serves 4

Put the oil in a large, non-stick skillet and set over high heat. Add the shallots, broccoli, and mushrooms and stir-fry for 3–4 minutes, until the mushrooms are soft and the broccoli turns a bright, emerald green. Add the spinach and cook until just wilted. Add the soy sauce and stir. Arrange the cubes of tofu over the vegetables so that they are evenly spaced. Preheat the broiler to high. Pour the beaten eggs into the skillet and cook over high heat until the edges have puffed up.

Keep the omelet in the skillet, place it under the preheated broiler and cook until golden and firm on top. Remove and let cool a little before drizzling with the oyster sauce (if using), then sprinkle with pepper to serve.

See photograph on page 55.

asparagus, corn, and goat cheese frittata

The frittata is a brilliant stand-by for a no-fuss, fast supper. It's an Italian-style omelet, often cooked slowly and still slightly moist when served, but I like to eat mine a little firmer, so flash it under a hot broiler. Crunchy asparagus and corn work nicely here combined with farm-fresh eggs, creamy goat cheese, and tangy fresh dill.

2 bunches of thin asparagus spears
kernels from 2 ears of corn, about 1½ cups
3 tablespoons butter
4 scallions, finely chopped
1 handful of fresh dill, chopped
8 eggs, beaten
7 oz. firm goat cheese, broken into pieces
sea salt and freshly ground black pepper

Serves 4

Trim, or snap off, the woody ends from the asparagus and cut the spears into 1-inch pieces.

Heat half of the butter in a large non-stick skillet set over medium heat. Add the asparagus, corn, and scallions and sauté for 2–3 minutes, stirring often. Transfer the vegetables to a large bowl and add the dill, reserving a little to use as garnish. Wipe the pan clean. Add the beaten eggs to the vegetables, gently stirring to combine, and season well with salt and pepper.

Preheat the broiler to high. Put the remaining butter in the skillet and set over high heat. Swirl the skillet around as the butter melts so that it coats the bottom and just starts to sizzle. Pour the frittata mixture into the skillet and reduce the heat to medium. Arrange the pieces of goat cheese over the top of the frittata and gently push them into the mixture. Cook for about 8 minutes, until the sides of the frittata start to puff up (reduce the heat if the bottom appears to be cooking too quickly).

Keep the fritatta in the skillet and place it under the preheated broiler. Cook for 1 minute only just to set the top. Let cool a little in the skillet, sprinkle with the reserved dill and serve immediately.

farfalle pasta with asparagus, soft-boiled duck eggs, and Parmesan

You can of course use hen's eggs here, but duck eggs are a bit of a treat and can easily be found at farmers' markets. They are slightly larger and have a rich flavor. They also make the best breakfast—simply soft-cooked and served with fingers of hot, buttered toast. Do use fine asparagus for this recipe; fresh and tender young spears that have been grown locally and haven't travelled too far would be best as, once picked, their sweetness fades fast.

4 duck eggs or 6 hen's eggs
2 bunches of thin asparagus spears
2 tablespoons olive oil
2 garlic cloves, chopped
1 cup light cream
14 oz. farfalle or other pasta of your choice
½ cup finely grated Parmesan cheese
2 handfuls of wild arugula leaves
sea salt and freshly ground black pepper

Serves 4

Put the eggs in a saucepan and pour in sufficient cold water to cover. Bring to a boil over high heat and cook for 5 minutes. Drain and run the eggs under cold water until the shells are cool enough to handle. Set aside.

Trim or snap any woody ends off the asparagus and cut the spears into 1 inch lengths. Put the oil in a saucepan and set over high heat. Add the asparagus and cook for 2 minutes, stirring constantly. Add the garlic and cook for another minute, then add the cream to the pan. Remove from the heat and let sit so that the garlic flavors the cream.

Cook the farfalle according to the package instructions. Drain and return it to the warm pan with the asparagus sauce. Peel and roughly chop the eggs. The yolks will be soft, so quickly add these to the warm pasta with the Parmesan and arugula. Season well with salt and pepper and stir gently to combine. Serve immediately.

mushrooms with bay leaves and lemon on toast

At farmers' markets you will often see a stall that sells just mushrooms. This is because they require unique growing conditions and many growers will dedicate themselves to growing nothing else—these guys really know their mushrooms! I use meaty cremini mushrooms here, as they keep their shape when cooked and can hold their own against the quietly intense flavor of bay leaves.

2 tablespoons light olive oil
2 bay leaves
2 strips of lemon zest
1 lb. large mushrooms, thinly sliced
2 garlic cloves, sliced
1 handful of fresh flat-leaf parsley, chopped
1 tablespoon freshly squeezed lemon juice
4 slices of sourdough bread, lightly toasted
sea salt and freshly ground black pepper

Serves 4

Put the oil in a skillet and set it over high heat. Add the mushrooms and cook for 8–10 minutes, turning them often. Add the bay leaves and lemon zest to the pan and cook for 1 minute to just flavor the mushrooms. Add the garlic and parsley, stir and cook for 1 minute, making sure that the garlic does not burn. Add the lemon juice and season well with salt and pepper.

Spoon the mushroom mixture onto the slices of toasted sourdough bread and serve immediately.

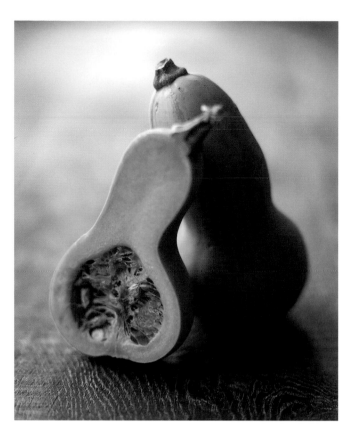

spaghetti with butternut squash, sage, and pecorino

¼ cup light olive oil

14 oz. butternut squash, peeled, seeded, and cut into thin wedges

2 garlic cloves, chopped

10–12 small fresh sage leaves

14 oz. spaghetti

1 handful of fresh flat-leaf parsley, chopped

½ cup Pecorino Romano cheese, grated

sea salt and freshly ground black pepper

Serves 4

This tasty pasta is inspired by the classic Italian dish of pumpkin-filled ravioli with sage butter except this is my inside-out version and therefore much easier to make! I've used butternut squash here, but you could use any winter squash, including pumpkin.

Put the oil in a skillet and set over high heat. Add the squash and cook for 5–6 minutes, turning often, until golden but not breaking up. Add the garlic and sage to the pan and cook for 2–3 minutes. Remove from the heat and let sit to allow the flavors to develop.

Cook the pasta according to the package instructions. Drain well and return to the warm pan with the squash mixture. Add the parsley and half of the Pecorino and season well with salt and pepper. Serve immediately with the remaining cheese sprinkled over the top.

soups and stews

roasted vegetable stock

I have often been disappointed with vegetable stock made in the classic way. Roasted vegetables are more flavorsome, so I prefer to use these as a base for stock. It's not necessary to follow this recipe to the letter. You could add almost anything you have to hand to this basic stock—some leftover tomato stalks, the green parts of leeks you usually discard, mushroom stems, even parsley stalks left over over when you have used just the leaves for a recipe.

3 tablespoons light olive oil
4–6 garlic cloves, unpeeled
2 large, ripe tomatoes, roughly chopped
2 leeks, sliced
2 carrots, chopped
3 celery ribs, chopped
1 fennel bulb, chopped
4 cremini mushrooms
1 bunch of fresh parsley stalks
1 tablespoon black peppercorns
sea salt (optional)

Makes about 1 litre

Preheat the oven to 350ºF. Put the oil and garlic in a roasting pan and heat in the oven for 10 minutes, until the oil is hot. Carefully add the vegetables to the pan and toss until coated in the hot oil. Return the pan to the oven and roast the vegetables for 1 hour, then turn them and cook for a further 15–30 minutes.

Transfer the vegetables and any of the oil from the pan to a large saucepan and add the parsley ribs, peppercorns, and 3 quarts cold water. Bring to a boil, then reduce the heat and let gently simmer for about 45 minutes. Pass the mixture through a fine strainer and add a little salt if liked.

The stock will keep for up to 5 days in an airtight container stored in the fridge or it can be frozen.

roasted tomato soup with rarebit toasts

The tomato is held in high regard in the Mediterranean countries, where a second-rate tomato is simply not an option! Many dishes that feature them have few other ingredients, so it's essential that the tomatoes themselves taste good. Dishes such as the Italian salad panzanella need not only the flesh but the juice of ripe tomatoes for the dressing, and Spanish salmorejo, a cold tomato and bread soup, is dependent on the tastiest of the summer crop. Buy your tomatoes in summer from a farmers' market and you can be assured of their quality.

2¼ lbs. Italian tomatoes, such as Roma, halved
2 small red onions, quartered
6 sprigs of fresh lemon thyme
1 teaspoon white sugar
1 teaspoon sea salt
2 garlic cloves, sliced
2 tablespoons olive oil
2 cups vegetable stock
sea salt and freshly ground black pepper

rarebit toast fingers:
4 oz. sharp cheddar cheese, grated
3 tablespoons wheat beer
1 tablespoon Worcestershire sauce
4 slices of whole-wheat bread or baguette

Serves 4

Preheat the oven to 325ºF. Put the tomatoes, onion, lemon thyme, sugar, salt, garlic, and oil in a large bowl. Use your hands to toss the ingredients to combine and evenly coat them in the oil. Tip the mixture out onto a baking sheet and roast in the preheated oven for 1½ hours. Discard the lemon thyme sprigs then put the tomatoes, onions, and any tasty juices in a food processor or blender and process until smooth, adding a little stock if the mixture is too thick to process. Transfer to a large saucepan, add the stock, and cook over gentle heat for 10 minutes. Season to taste and keep warm.

Preheat the broiler to high. Put the grated cheddar, beer, and Worcestershire sauce in a small saucepan set over low heat. Stir until the cheese has melted and the mixture is smooth. Toast the bread under the preheated broiler on one side only. Spread about 2 tablespoons of the cheese mixture on each untoasted side of bread and broil until it is bubbling and golden. Cut into fingers and serve with the soup.

Buying locally grown or sourced foods is today's message but it has actually been over 30 years since chef Alice Waters pioneered this philosophy by using her Berkeley restaurant to promote organic and small farm products, and in doing so helped to establish farmers' markets throughout the Bay Area, and eventually the rest of the country. This ethos resonates here in this simple recipe—to really savor its delightful sweetness, corn should be eaten really fresh, so do try and get your hands on fresh ears still wrapped in their husks and no more than a day or two from the field.

summer corn soup

kernels from 8 ears of corn, about 6 cups
1 onion, chopped
1 celery rib, chopped
2 garlic cloves, chopped
3 tablespoons butter
6 cups vegetable stock
½ cup light cream
Red Bell Pepper Tapenade (see page 35), to serve (optional)
1 small bunch of fresh chives, snipped
sea salt and freshly ground black pepper
crusty bread, to serve

Serves 4

Put the corn, onion, celery, garlic, and butter in a large saucepan and season well with salt and pepper. Set over medium heat and partially cover with a lid. Cook for 10 minutes, shaking the pan often. Add the stock, bring to a boil and let boil for 15 minutes. Remove from the heat and let cool for about 20 minutes.

Transfer the mixture to a food processor or blender and whizz until smooth. You may need to do this in batches. Force the mixture through a fine strainer and return it to a clean saucepan. Add the cream and gently reheat, stirring constantly.

Ladle the soup into warmed serving bowls, top with a dollop of Red Bell Pepper Tapenade (if using), sprinkle with chives, and serve with thick slices of good, crusty bread.

slow-cooked onion and cider soup with Gruyère toasts

I couldn't begin to imagine cooking without onions—they are so versatile. The soft and sweet onion mixture here could be added to an egg custard and baked in a pastry shell with some soft goat cheese to make a savory tart, or spread on a pizza base and topped with black olives and fresh thyme for a classic French pissaladière.

3 tablespoons butter
2¼ lbs. yellow onions, sliced
4 garlic cloves
4 cups vegetable stock
1½ cups hard cider
2 egg yolks
4 thin slices of baguette or similar
4 oz. Gruyère cheese, thinly sliced

Serves 4

Put the butter in a saucepan set over medium heat. Add the onions and garlic, partially cover with a lid and cook for 20 minutes, stirring often so that the onions become silky soft without burning. Add the stock and cider and bring to a boil. Reduce heat to low and cook for 40 minutes, until the soup is thick and golden. Remove from the heat and slowly whisk in the egg yolks. Cover and keep warm.

Preheat the broiler to high. Toast the bread under the hot broiler until lightly golden on one side only. Put the Gruyère slices on the untoasted side and cook under the broiler until the cheese is golden brown and bubbling. Ladle the soup into warmed serving bowls and sit a Gruyère toast on top of each to serve.

barley risotto with collard greens and radicchio

You will often see collard greens and radicchio displayed side by side at farmers' markets—both look appealing, especially the boldly colored radicchio, the "painted lady" of the lettuce world. When used raw in salads it can be a little too bitter for my liking, but when cooked in this risotto its flavor is softened and the barley adds a nice nutty note.

1¼ cups pearl barley
2 tablespoons light olive oil
1 lb. collard greens, roughly chopped
4 large radicchio leaves, torn
finely grated zest and freshly squeezed juice of 1 unwaxed lemon
5 cups vegetable stock
2 tablespoons butter
1 leek, thinly sliced
2 garlic cloves, chopped
2 teaspoons fresh thyme leaves
1 tablespoon fresh rosemary needles
½ cup finely grated Parmesan cheese, plus extra to serve
1 handful of fresh flat-leaf parsley, chopped

Serves 4

Put the barley in a large, heatproof bowl and add sufficient boiling water to cover. Let sit for 10 minutes, just to soften the barley a little, then drain well and set aside.

Put the oil in a skillet set over medium heat. Add the collard greens and radicchio and cook for 10 minutes, stirring often, until the leaves soften. Add the lemon zest and juice, stir well and set aside. Put the stock in a large saucepan set over low heat and gently warm through while you start the risotto.

Put half of the butter in a saucepan set over medium heat. Add the leek and garlic and cook for 4–5 minutes until the leeks are soft and silky. Add the barley and herbs and stir for 1 minute. Add a ladleful of the warmed stock and cook, stirring constantly, until almost all the stock has been absorbed. Repeat the process until all the stock has been incorporated and the barley is almost cooked through—the risotto will be quite wet. Add the collard greens, radicchio, remaining butter, and Parmesan to the pan and stir well to combine. Sprinkle with the parsley and serve with extra Parmesan on the side for sprinkling.

See photograph on page 70.

miso with ramen noodles and stir-fried vegetables

Japanese broths are hearty and comforting. They are often full of fresh and earthy cold-weather vegetables, sometimes with the addition of fresh corn. The broths themselves are generally made with a base of simple stock and soy sauce or miso. This prepared, soybean paste is probably the most essential Japanese food item with a very strong "unami" (savory) flavor component. Easily found in the Asian foods aisle at your supermarket or a speciality food store, it will keep for ages in your refrigerator. The noodles, although common in Japan, are Chinese wheat-based noodles and, when bought dried, are a very useful pantry staple.

3 tablespoons red miso paste
1 tablespoon light soy sauce
½ teaspoon white sugar
1.25 litres vegetable stock
7 oz. ramen or thin egg noodles
1 tablespoon light olive oil
2 teaspoons sesame oil
2 teaspoons finely sliced fresh ginger
2 shallots, thinly sliced
2 leeks, julienned
7 oz. Savoy cabbage leaves, finely shredded
7 oz. red cabbage, finely shredded

Serves 4

Combine the miso, soy sauce, sugar, and stock in a large saucepan set over medium heat and warm until the miso has completely dissolved. Keep warm over low heat. Cook the noodles according to the packet directions. Drain well and divide between 4 warmed serving bowls.

Put the oils in a wok or large skillet set over high heat. Add the ginger and shallots and cook for just a few seconds to flavor the oil. Add the leeks and cabbage and stir-fry for 2 minutes, until the vegetables are crisp and glistening with oil.

Ladle the warm miso mixture over the noodles and top with the stir-fried vegetables. Serve immediately.

See photograph on page 71.

smoky hotpot of great northern beans

This is a hearty hotpot packed with fall vegetables and rich with smoky paprika. Great northern beans are large and white, resembling lima beans in shape but with a distinctive, delicate flavor. They are widely grown in Midwest America, where they are used in baked dishes. If you can't find them, large lima beans will do just as well.

½ cup dried great northern or lima beans
2 tablespoons olive oil
1 large onion, chopped
2 garlic cloves, chopped
2 teaspoons smoked Spanish paprika (pimentón)
1 celery rib, chopped
1 carrot, chopped
2 medium waxy potatoes, cut into 1-inch dice
1 red bell pepper, chopped
2 cups vegetable stock
sea salt and freshly ground black pepper
crusty bread, to serve

Serves 4

Soak the dried beans in cold water for at least 6 hours or ideally overnight. Drain and put in a large saucepan with sufficient just-boiled water to cover. Cook for 30 minutes until softened. Drain and set aside until needed.

Put the oil in a saucepan set over medium heat. Add the onion and cook for 4–5 minutes until softened. Add the garlic and paprika to the pan and stir-fry for 2 minutes. Add the celery, carrot, potatoes, and red bell pepper and cook for 2 minutes, stirring constantly to coat the vegetables in the flavored oil. Add the stock and beans and bring to a boil. Reduce the heat and partially cover the pan with a lid. Let simmer for 40 minutes, stirring often, until all the vegetables are cooked. Season to taste and serve with crusty bread for dipping in the sauce.

This technique of cooking rice is a particular favorite of mine. Although Middle Eastern in origin, it has spread far and wide—similar rice dishes can be found in European, Asian, Latin American, Caribbean, and Indian cuisines, and it is known by many names including pilaf, pilav, and pulao.

orange vegetable and scallion pilau

2 tablespoons light olive oil

1 onion, chopped

2 garlic cloves, chopped

1 tablespoon finely grated fresh ginger

1 large red chile, finely chopped

1 teaspoon ground coriander

1 teaspoon ground cumin

1 teaspoon turmeric

½ cup slivered almonds

1½ cups basmati rice

1 carrot, cut into large chunks

7 oz. pumpkin or squash, peeled, seeded, and cut into wedges

1 small sweet potato, peeled and cut into thick half-circles

freshly squeezed juice of 1 lime

1 handful of fresh cilantro leaves, chopped

Serves 4

Put the oil in a heavy-based saucepan set over high heat. Add the onion, garlic, ginger, and chile and cook for 5 minutes, stirring often. Add the spices and almonds and cook for a further 5 minutes, until the spices become aromatic and look very dark in the pan.

Add the rice and cook for a minute, stirring well to coat the rice in the spices. Add the carrot, pumpkin, and sweet potato to the pan. Pour in 2½ cups water and stir well, loosening any grains of rice that are stuck to the bottom of the pan. Bring to a boil, then reduce the heat to low, cover the pan with a tight-fitting lid, and cook for 25 minutes, stirring occasionally.

Add the lime juice and cilantro, stir well to combine and serve.

I like to define minestrone as a hodgepodge of whatever strikes your fancy. Often thought of as cold weather fare, this version has summer written all over it and is packed with fresh tomatoes and green beans as well as chickpeas, a staple my pantry would never be without. As if it weren't already summery enough, I have added a few handfuls of arugula. Its peppery bite and fresh taste lightens the soup, while making it much more than just another minestrone.

chickpea, tomato, and green bean minestrone

2 tablespoons olive oil

1 onion, chopped

2 garlic cloves, chopped

14-oz can chickpeas, rinsed and drained

4 oz. green beans, sliced at an angle

6 ripe tomatoes, halved

1 handful of chopped fresh flat-leaf parsley

6 cups vegetable stock

3½ oz. whole-wheat spaghetti, broken into 2-inch pieces

2 handfuls of arugula

½ cup finely grated Pecorino Romano or Parmesan cheese, finely grated

sea salt and freshly ground black pepper

crusty bread, to serve

Serves 4

Put the oil in a large saucepan set over medium heat. Add the onion, partially cover with a lid and cook for 4–5 minutes, stirring often, until softened. Add the garlic and cook for 1 minute. Add the chickpeas, green beans, tomatoes, parsley, stock, and spaghetti and bring to a boil.

Reduce the heat and let simmer for 40 minutes, stirring often, until the pasta is cooked and the soup is thick. Season to taste with salt and pepper.

Just before serving, add the arugula and gently stir until the arugula softens. Ladle into warmed serving bowls and sprinkle a generous amount of grated Pecorino over the top. Serve immediately with chunks of crusty bread.

Next time: Try making this delicious soup with different vegetables. Zucchini and carrots are a nice addition but remember that both take a little longer to cook so dice them very finely before adding to the soup with the other vegetables. A pinch of smoky Spanish paprika (pimentón) will add a slightly different flavor.

sweet potato and coconut soup with Thai pesto

Sweet potatoes make an excellent ingredient for soups. When blended they take on a velvety, creamy texture. Here, their sweetness is cut through with some full-on and spicy Asian flavors in the form of a Thai-style pesto, which really brings this soup to life.

1 tablespoon light olive oil

1 lb. sweet potatoes, peeled and chopped into chunks

1 red onion, chopped

1 tablespoon Thai red curry paste

2 cups vegetable stock

2 cups coconut milk

Thai pesto:

⅔ cup unsalted peanuts, lightly toasted

2 garlic cloves, chopped

2 teaspoons finely grated fresh ginger

2 large green chiles, seeded and chopped

1 small bunch of fresh cilantro

1 large handful of fresh mint leaves

1 large handful of fresh basil leaves

2 tablespoons light soy sauce or Thai fish sauce

2 tablespoons freshly squeezed lime juice

1 tablespoon soft light brown sugar

Serves 4

Put the oil in a heavy-based saucepan set over medium heat. Add the sweet potatoes and onion, partially cover with a lid, and cook for 15 minutes, stirring often, until they are soft and just starting to turn golden. Increase the heat to high, add the curry paste, and stir-fry for 3–4 minutes so that the paste cooks and becomes fragrant. Add the stock and coconut milk and bring to a boil. Transfer the mixture to a food processor or blender and whizz until smooth. Return the soup to a clean saucepan.

To make the pesto, put all of the ingredients in a food processor or blender and whizz, occasionally scraping down the sides of the bowl, until you have a chunky green paste and the ingredients are all evenly chopped. Gently reheat the soup, then ladle into warmed serving bowls. Top with a generous spoonful of Thai pesto to serve.

spiced cauliflower with red bell pepper and peas

I think that the vegetarian recipes you find in Indian cuisine are some of the most delicious in the world. Many of the recipes seem to embrace my philosophy of cooking fresh produce at its best, keeping it simple, and letting the flavors speak for themselves—good honest cooking. This is a spicy treat that's perfect if you like things hot.

½ head of cauliflower, cut into large florets

2 teaspoons ground cumin

1 teaspoon turmeric

3 tablespoons light olive oil

2 teaspoons black mustard seeds

6–8 curry leaves

1 onion, sliced

1 small red bell pepper, thinly sliced

1 tablespoon finely grated fresh ginger

2 garlic cloves, chopped

1 large green chile, sliced

½ cup vegetable stock

2 ripe tomatoes, chopped

1 cup shelled fresh peas

steamed or boiled basmati rice, to serve (optional)

Serves 4

Put the cauliflower florets in a large bowl with the cumin and turmeric and toss until evenly coated in the spices.

Put the oil in a skillet set over medium/high heat. Add the cauliflower, mustard seeds, and curry leaves and cook for 8–10 minutes, turning the pieces often so that they soften and color with the spices. Add the onion and red bell pepper and cook for 5 minutes. Add the ginger, garlic, and chile and stir-fry for 1 minute, then add the stock, tomatoes, and peas. Reduce the heat and let simmer gently for 10 minutes until the vegetables are tender and cooked through.

Spoon over basmati rice to serve, if liked.

See photograph on page 80.

creamy vegetable and cashew curry

The vibrant colors of Kerala, India's southern-most state, are all here on a plate. This deliciously creamy curry is made even richer with the addition of that irresistably delicious snack, the cashew nut.

2 tablespoons vegetable oil
¾ cup large, unsalted cashews
6 shallots, peeled and halved
1 teaspoon black mustard seeds
6–8 curry leaves
2 garlic cloves, chopped
1 tablespoon finely grated fresh ginger
1 teaspoon turmeric
4 large dried red chiles
1 small red bell pepper, thinly sliced
2 ripe tomatoes, quartered
8 very small new potatoes, halved
14-oz can coconut milk
steamed or boiled basmati rice, to serve (optional)

Serves 4

Put the oil in a heavy-based saucepan set over medium heat. Add the cashews and shallots and cook for 5 minutes, stirring often, until the cashew are just starting to brown. Add the mustard seeds and curry leaves and cook until the seeds start to pop. Add the garlic, ginger, turmeric, chiles, and red bell pepper to the pan and stir-fry for 2 minutes, until aromatic.

Add the tomatoes, potatoes, and coconut milk, partially cover the pan and let simmer gently over low heat for about 20 minutes, or until the potatoes are cooked through. Spoon over basmati rice to serve, if liked.

See photograph on page 81.

Napolitana lentil stew

I use the term Napolitana here to loosely describe the predominance of tomatoes in this Mediterranean-style stew although the flavors could easily be described as Greek, given the inclusion of fresh oregano and feta. There are few ingredients in this dish, so the tomatoes must be of premium quality and vine-ripened in the summer sun.

½ cup green or brown lentils
3 tablespoons olive oil
1 onion, chopped
2 garlic cloves, chopped
a small handful of fresh oregano, chopped
1 teaspoon dried hot pepper flakes
1½ tablespoons salted caperberries, rinsed
2 ripe tomatoes, roughly chopped
1 cup passata or tomato purée
2 oz. small black olives
4 oz. feta cheese, crumbled
crusty bread, to serve

Serves 4

Put the lentils in a large saucepan, add sufficient cold water to cover and set over high heat. Bring to a boil, then reduce the heat and let simmer for 20 minutes until the lentils are tender but retain a little "bite". Drain and set aside until needed.

Put the oil in a saucepan set over high heat. Add the onion, garlic, oregano, and pepper flakes and cook for 5 minutes, stirring often, until the onion softens. Add the capers, tomatoes, passata, lentils, and 1 cup water. Bring to a boil, then reduce the heat and let simmer gently for 10 minutes, stirring occasionally.

Spoon into warmed serving dishes, top with the olives and crumbled feta and serve with crusty bread on the side for dipping into the rich sauce.

Eggplant is probably the vegetable I cook with most often, as it works so well with all of my favorite Asian and Mediterranean flavors. So many iconic international meat-free dishes are based on eggplant, such as the spicy Middle Eastern dip baba ghanoush, Sicilian caponata, and the French classic ratatouille. I also like color in food and this recipe does not disappoint on that score.

eggplant, tomato, and red lentil curry

3 tablespoons light olive oil

1 large eggplant, cut into 8 pieces

1 red onion, chopped

2 garlic cloves, chopped

1 tablespoon finely chopped fresh ginger

8 oz. cherry tomatoes on the vine

6–8 curry leaves

1 teaspoon ground cumin

¼ teaspoon chili powder

1 tablespoon tomato paste

⅔ cup red split lentils

1 handful of fresh cilantro, roughly chopped

boiled or steamed basmati rice, to serve (optional)

Serves 4

Heat the oil in a skillet set over high heat. When the oil is smoking hot add the eggplant to the skillet and cook for 5 minutes, turning the pieces often so that they cook evenly. At first the eggplant will absorb the oil, but as it cooks to a dark and golden color, the oil will start to seep out back into the skillet. Remove the eggplant from the skillet at this point and not before.

Add the remaining oil, onions, garlic, and ginger to the pan and cook for 5 minutes. Add the cherry tomatoes and cook for 1 minute, until they just soften and collapse, then remove them from the skillet before they break up too much and set aside with the eggplant.

Add the curry leaves and cumin to the pan and cook for a couple of minutes as the curry leaves pop and crackle. Add the chili powder, tomato paste, 2 cups water and the lentils and simmer for 15–20 minutes, until the lentils are tender but retain some "bite". Stir in the eggplant and cherry tomatoes and cook the curry for a couple of minutes just to warm through. Stir in the cilantro and spoon over basmati rice to serve, if liked.

saturday night
dinners

antipasto sharing plate

These delicious Italian-style antipasti are the perfect solution to entertaining friends. The Italians have a special way with vegetables—no wonder, when their produce is so ripe and full of flavor. Serve this sharing plate with a selection of tasty Italian breads and some fruity olive oil for dipping.

marinated mushrooms

2 cups dry white wine
1 cup white wine vinegar
2 bay leaves
1 teaspoon white sugar
1 lb. button mushrooms
2 tablespoons olive oil
1 garlic clove, crushed
1 teaspoon finely grated lemon zest from an unwaxed lemon
2 tablespoons freshly squeezed lemon juice
½ teaspoon dried hot pepper flakes
1 handful of fresh flat-leaf parsley leaves, chopped
sea salt

Serves 6–8 sharing

Put the wine and vinegar in a large saucepan set over high heat and add the bay leaves, sugar, and 1 teaspoon salt. Bring to a boil, add the mushrooms and let them poach in the hot liquid for 4–5 minutes. Remove with a slotted spoon and drain on paper towels. Put the mushrooms in a bowl.

Combine the oil, garlic, lemon zest, and juice, pepper flakes, and parsley in a bowl and pour over the mushrooms while they are still warm. Cover and let sit for at least 3 hours to allow the flavors to develop, stirring often. Season to taste with salt before serving.

wilted spinach with fried garlic

2¼ lbs. fresh baby spinach leaves
¼ cup light olive oil
6 garlic cloves, thinly sliced
sea salt and freshly ground black pepper

Serves 6–8 sharing

Bring a large saucepan of lightly salted water to a boil and add the spinach. Cook for 1 minute, until the leaves wilt and turn emerald green. Drain and rinse with cold running water. Drain well and use your hands to squeeze out as much liquid as possible then transfer to a bowl. Heat the oil in a skillet set over medium/high heat. When the oil starts to smoke, remove the pan from the heat and add the garlic, stirring constantly, until it turns golden. Pour the oil and fried garlic over the spinach and toss to coat evenly in the oil. Season well with salt and pepper. Let sit for about 20 minutes to allow the flavors to develop before serving.

smoky eggplant dip

1 large eggplant
½ cup Greek yogurt
1 teaspoon ground cumin
1 tablespoon freshly squeezed lemon juice
1 teaspoon sea salt
½ teaspoon ground white pepper
smoked Spanish paprika (pimentón), for sprinkling

Preheat the oven to 425°F. Prick the eggplant all over with the prongs of a fork. Sit it on the middle shelf of the preheated oven and bake for about 15 minutes, turning once or twice, until the skin is puffed up all over. Let the eggplant sit until it has collapsed and softened.

When cool enough to handle, peel off the skin (leaving a few small charred bits to add a smoky flavor). Put the flesh in a food processor and add the yogurt, cumin, lemon juice, salt and pepper and process until smooth. Transfer to a serving bowl and sprinkle with paprika to serve.

baked squash blossoms

½ cup fresh ricotta cheese
¼ cup soft feta cheese
1 teaspoon fresh thyme leaves
12 small squash blossoms
2 tablespoons olive oil
2 teaspoons freshly squeezed lemon juice
sea salt and freshly ground black pepper

Makes 12

Preheat the oven to 350°F and lightly oil an ovenproof baking dish. Put the ricotta and feta in a bowl and add the thyme. Season well with salt and pepper. Carefully separate the petals of the squash blossoms and pick out the stamens. Put about 1 teaspoon of the cheese mixture into each flower and bring the petals together, gently twisting them to seal the cheese inside. Put the flowers in the baking dish so that they fit snugly and drizzle over the oil and lemon juice. Bake in the preheated oven for about 15–20 minutes until the stems have softened and the cheese is starting to ooze out. Serve immediately or they will spoil.

A Greek salad is a bit like any other iconic salad in that everyone has their own version. In my recipe the feta cheese is kept separate and used only in the creamy dressing. The dressing is also great served with simply broiled or grilled vegetables or as dip for crunchy, raw vegetables such as bell peppers, carrots, and celery. Lavash is a Lebanese flatbread—if you can't easily find it, use Greek-style pita bread instead.

Greek salad with creamy feta dressing and lavash crisps

7 oz. lavash or pita bread, torn into pieces

1 lb. mixed, ripe tomatoes, large ones cut into bite-size pieces

1 small red bell pepper, thinly sliced

1 small yellow bell pepper, thinly sliced

1 cucumber, sliced

1 red onion, thinly sliced

3 oz. small black olives

2 handfuls of fresh mint leaves

3 tablespoons olive oil

creamy feta dressing:

3½ oz. feta cheese, crumbled

2 garlic cloves, crushed

1 tablespoon white wine vinegar

1 tablespoon finely chopped fresh dill

3 tablepoons light olive oil

½ cup whole milk

Serves 4

To make the dressing, put the feta, garlic, vinegar, dill, and oil in a food processor or blender and whizz until the mixture is well combined and thick. With the motor still running, add the milk in a steady stream until the mixture is smooth and creamy. Do not overmix. Set the dressing aside until needed.

Preheat the oven to 325°F. Put the lavash pieces on a baking sheet and bake in the preheated oven for 10 minutes. Transfer to a wire rack, arranging them in a single layer, and let cool.

Put the tomatoes, bell peppers, cucumber, onion, olives, mint, and oil in a large bowl and gently toss to combine. Just before serving, add the lavash crisps, toss again and serve with the feta dressing on the side for drizzling.

chile-roasted vegetables with soft goat cheese

This is a stunning summer dish and I get hungry just thinking about it! Any bell peppers will do, but the pointed, slightly smaller Ramiro peppers work particularly well because of their sweeter flesh. Once cooked, let this sit at room temperature for a short while so that all the lovely flavors meld together and the cheese marinates in the juices. Slices of toasted or wood-fired bread really set this off nicely.

4 small red or yellow bell peppers, sliced

1 fennel bulb, thinly sliced and fronds chopped

8 ripe tomatoes, halved

2 garlic cloves, thinly sliced

2 large red chiles, seeded and thinly sliced

1 teaspoon sea salt

¼ cup olive oil

7 oz. soft goat cheese, sliced

a small handful of fresh basil leaves

2 tablespoons balsamic vinegar

toasted sourdough bread, to serve

Serves 4

Preheat the oven to 350°F. Put the bell peppers, fennel, fennel fronds, tomatoes, garlic, and chiles in a large bowl with the salt and oil. Toss until evenly coated in the oil and arrange in a roasting pan. Roast in the preheated oven for about 1 hour, turning once after about 30 minutes, until the vegetables are just starting to blacken around the edges. Remove from the oven and let cool for 20–30 minutes

Lift the still-warm vegetables onto a large serving plate, reserving the cooking juices. Top with the cheese and basil leaves. Mix the reserved juices with the vinegar and spoon over the salad. Let sit for a little while before serving at room temperature, with toasted sourdough bread for mopping up the delicious juices.

tomato and mozzarella salad with eggplant relish

This eggplant relish takes its cue from the popular Sicilian side dish caponata—a combination of summer vegetables with olives and caperberries, gently spiked with wine vinegar. Left to cool, its bittersweet flavor intensifies and makes it the perfect partner for creamy buffalo mozzarella.

6 mixed ripe tomatoes, thinly sliced

3 large balls of fresh buffalo mozzarella, torn

eggplant relish:

1 medium eggplant, cut into small cubes

1 teaspoon salt

⅓ cup light olive oil

1 red onion, finely diced

2 garlic cloves, chopped

1 celery rib, finely diced

1 small red bell pepper, finely diced

1 tablespoon small salted caperberries, rinsed

3 oz. small black olives

¼ cup red wine vinegar

2 teaspoons white sugar

a handful of fresh mint leaves, finely sliced

sea salt and freshly ground black pepper

Serves 4

To make the relish, put the eggplant in a colander with the salt and use your hands to toss together. Let sit for 30 minutes, then using your hands, squeeze out as much liquid from the eggplant as you can, without squashing the flesh too much.

Put the oil in a skillet set over high heat. Add the onion and cook for 2 minutes. Add the eggplant and cook for 8–10 minutes, stirring often, until the eggplant turns golden. Add the garlic and cook for 1 minute only—don't let the garlic burn. Add the celery, red bell pepper, caperberries, and olives and stir-fry for just 1 minute so that the vegetables stay crisp. Add the vinegar and sugar to the skillet and bring to a boil, cooking for 1 minute. Remove from the heat and season to taste with salt and pepper. Let sit at room temperature for at least 30 minutes to allow the flavors to develop.

Arrange the tomato slices on a large serving plate and scatter the mozzarella pieces over the top. Spoon over the eggplant relish and sprinkle with the mint leaves to serve.

See photograph on page 94.

pasta primavera with lemony bread crumbs

This light Italian pasta dish can be made using just about any crisp, green veggies you find at the spring farmers' markets, such as green beans, peas, and young zucchini.

4 tablespoons light olive oil

1 cup fresh white bread crumbs

1 tablespoon finely grated zest from an unwaxed lemon

1 tablespoon fresh thyme leaves

½ cup finely grated Parmesan cheese

1 cup peas (frozen or freshly shelled)

⅔ cup green beans

1 bunch of baby asparagus, sliced at an angle

2 small zucchini, cut into matchsticks

2 garlic cloves, chopped

2 ripe tomatoes, peeled, seeded, and chopped

14 oz. spaghetti or tagliatelle

sea salt and freshly ground black pepper

Serves 4

Put half of the oil in a skillet set over medium heat. Add the bread crumbs, lemon zest, and thyme and cook for 4–5 minutes, stirring constantly, shaking the skillet so that the bread crumbs turn an even golden color. Add 1 tablespoon of the Parmesan and stir until combined. Remove the mixture from the skillet and set aside.

Bring a large saucepan of lightly salted water to a boil and add the peas, beans, asparagus, and zucchini. Cook for 2 minutes to just blanch and drain well. Heat the remaining oil in a large skillet set over high heat, add the garlic, and cook for just a few seconds to flavor the oil. Add the tomatoes and cook for 1 minute, until they are softened.

Return the blanched vegetables to the skillet with the tomatoes, cook for 1–2 minutes, and cover to keep warm. Cook the pasta according to the package directions. Drain well and return it to the warm skillet. Add the vegetable and tomato mixture and half the lemony bread crumbs and stir gently to combine. Season well with salt and pepper. Spoon onto serving plates and sprinkle with the remaining lemony bread crumbs and Parmesan to serve.

See photograph on page 95.

peppery watercress and pea soup with Gorgonzola

Despite taking no time at all to prepare, there is something about watercress soup that seems quintessentially English and refined. Its mustardy bite sits nicely with the intensely flavored Gorgonzola. Serve this as an appetizer when you want to make a good impression.

1 small bunch of watercress, about 10 oz.

3 tablespoons butter

1 onion, chopped

1 celery rib, chopped

4 oz. arugula

½ teaspoon cracked black pepper

2 cups peas (frozen or freshly shelled)

6 cups vegetable stock

4 oz. Gorgonzola cheese (optional)

Serves 4

Pick over the watercress to remove any discolored leaves. Cut off and discard about 2 inches from the bottom of the stems. Roughly chop the leaves and remaining stems and set aside.

Put the butter in a large saucepan set over high heat and melt until sizzling. Add the onion and celery and cook for 2–3 minutes, until softened. Add the watercress, arugula, and pepper and stir-fry for a couple of minutes until the greens wilt and start to pop in the hot pan. Add the peas and stock and bring to a boil. Reduce the heat and cook at a rapid simmer for 10 minutes, until all the vegetables are very soft. Transfer the mixture to a food processor or blender and whizz until smooth. Pass the mixture through a sieve into a clean saucepan and gently reheat.

Cut the Gorgonzola into 4 pieces (if using) and put 1 in the bottom of each of 4 warmed serving bowls. Ladle the hot soup over the top and serve immediately.

In Provençal dialect, pistou literally means "pounded" and it's a highly appropriate name for this classic French sauce, which is made by crushing the ingredients in a mortar with a pestle. The resulting paste, similar in style to an Italian pesto, is then traditionally stirred into a rich vegetable soup to amplify its flavor. Just like a homemade pesto, pistou is best eaten as soon as possible, as it quickly becomes bitter. Try and find tender young fava beans for this light, broth-style soup—older beans will have tough skins and need to be shelled.

summer vegetable soup with pasta and pistou

2 tablespoons light olive oil

6 baby leeks, finely sliced

2 zucchini, cut into large dice

2 small yellow pattypan squash

1 small fennel bulb, cut into large dice

4 cups vegetable stock

4 oz. young pea pods

4 oz. fresh fava beans, shelled if necessary

2 oz. fresh pasta shape of your choice

freshly grated Parmesan cheese, to serve

pistou:

4 garlic cloves, chopped

½ teaspoon sea salt

2 tomatoes, peeled, seeded, and chopped

2 cups fresh basil leaves, roughly torn

1 cup fresh flat-leaf parsley leaves

½ cup olive oil

2 tablespoons freshly squeezed lemon juice

¼ cup finely grated Parmesan cheese

Serves 4

To make the pistou, put the garlic and salt in a large mortar and pound with a pestle until the garlic forms a smooth paste. Add the tomatoes and pound until smooth. Add the basil and parsley and pound until combined. Slowly add the olive oil until it is all incorporated. Add the lemon juice and Parmesan and stir to combine. Cover and refrigerate until needed.

Put the light olive oil in a large saucepan set over high heat. Add the leeks and cook for 2–3 minutes, stirring constantly. Add the zucchini, squash, and fennel and cook, stirring, for 1–2 minutes until the vegetables soften but keep their color. Add the stock and bring to a boil. Add the pea pods and fava beans and cook for 5 minutes. Add the pasta to the soup and gently simmer for 1–2 minutes, it is cooked but still retains a little "bite".

Ladle into warmed serving bowls, top with a dollop of pistou, and sprinkle with Parmesan to serve.

Fresh chestnuts aren't always easy to find, but if you can get your hands on some, they really do make a wonderful addition to this pasta dish with a slightly festive flavor. Don't feel too guilty about the cream—the chestnuts are low in both fat and calories.

pappardelle pasta with portobello mushrooms, chestnuts, and chives

7 oz. fresh chestnuts (optional)

1 tablespoon olive oil

1 tablespoon butter

2 garlic cloves, chopped

14 oz. portobello mushrooms, sliced

2 fresh thyme sprigs

½ cup dry white wine

1 cup light cream

1 bunch of chives, cut into 1-inch lengths

2 oz. Pecorino Romano cheese, finely grated, plus extra to serve

14 oz. pappardelle, tagliatelle, or any other ribbon pasta

sea salt and freshly ground black pepper

Serves 4

Preheat the oven to 400°F. Score a cross on one end of each chestnut. Put them on a baking sheet and roast in the preheated oven for 10–15 minutes, until the skins split. Remove and let cool. When cool enough to handle, pull off the shells, and rub away the fleshy skin underneath. Set aside until needed.

Put the oil and butter in a skillet set over high heat. When the butter sizzles, add the garlic and cook for just 1 minute, making sure it doesn't burn. Add the mushrooms and thyme, reduce the heat to medium, and partially cover with a lid. Cook for 10 minutes, stirring often. Add the wine to the skillet and simmer until the liquid is reduced by half. Add the cream, reduce the heat, and cook for 15 minutes, until the mixture thickens. Add the chives and half of the Pecorino and stir to combine. Season to taste with salt and pepper. Cover with foil to keep warm.

Cook the pasta according to the package directions. Drain well and return to the warm pan. Add the mushroom sauce, gently toss to mix and serve immediately with extra Pecorino cheese for sprinkling.

root vegetable ragù with spiced couscous

This is a hearty dish packed with nutritious root veggies. This method for mawking couscous is not the traditional Moroccan way, but it does produce a full-flavored version that makes the perfect accompaniment to the ragù.

3 tablespoons olive oil

2 tablespoons butter

1 red onion, chopped

1 celery rib, roughly chopped

6 garlic cloves, lightly smashed

2 cups passata or tomato purée

2 cups vegetable stock

2 tablespoons fresh oregano leaves

1 parsnip, peeled and chopped

2 carrots, peeled and chopped

6 small, new potatoes

spiced cous cous:

1½ cups vegetable stock

2 tablespoons butter

2 cups couscous

1 teaspoon each of ground cumin, ground coriander, and smoky Spanish paprika (pimentón)

¼ teaspoon cayenne pepper

Serves 4

Put the oil and butter in a large saucepan set over high heat. When the butter sizzles, add the onion, celery, and garlic. Reduce heat to medium, partially cover the pan and cook for 10 minutes, stirring often, until the vegetables are soft and lightly browned. Add the passata, stock, and oregano and bring to a boil. Reduce the heat to a medium simmer and cook, uncovered, for about 20 minutes. Add the parsnip, carrots, and potatoes to the pan and cook for a further 15–20 minutes until tender.

To make the spiced couscous, put the stock and butter in a small saucepan set over high heat. Bring to a boil, then reduce the heat to low and keep the stock warm. Put the couscous and spices in a medium, heavy-based saucepan and cook over medium/high heat until the spices are aromatic and just start to turn a dusky brown. Turn off the heat. Pour the warm stock into the pan. Stir, cover with a tight-fitting lid, and let sit for 10 minutes. Fluff up the couscous with a fork, cover again and let sit for a further 5 minutes. Tip the couscous out into a bowl and fluff up to separate as many grains as possible. Spoon onto serving plates, top with the root vegetable ragù and serve.

globe artichoke, tarragon, and Roquefort soup

Artichokes can seem a little daunting, but in this recipe you don't have to worry about cutting out all of the fibrous, inedible bits—you just cook them until they are soft enough to remove. I'm always looking for ways to use tarragon, but it isn't easy, as its aromatic flavor can be a little overpowering. It works nicely here though, as does the Roquefort, making this a very special soup.

freshly squeezed juice of 1 lemon

8 large globe artichokes

1 tablespoon olive oil

2 tablespoons butter

1 large leek, sliced

1 garlic clove, chopped

2 tablespoons fresh tarragon leaves

2 cups vegetable stock

½ cup light cream

4 oz. Roquefort cheese, roughly crumbled

sea salt and freshly ground black pepper

Pumpkin and Caraway Seed Soda Bread (see page 36), to serve (optional)

Serves 4

Bring a large saucepan of water to a boil. Put the lemon juice and 6 cups water in a large bowl. Trim the leaves and stems from the artichokes. Cut each head in half and remove the hairy chokes. (Don't worry if you miss some of the gnarly bits, as they will come off more easily after cooking.) As you prepare each one, drop it in the bowl of water and lemon juice to prevent it from discoloring. When all the artichokes are prepared, add them to the pan of boiling water. Cook for 10–12 minutes and drain. Set aside. When cool enough to handle, trim the artichokes so that you are left with just the soft, fleshy bits.

Put the oil and butter in a large saucepan set over high heat. When the butter sizzles, add the leek and garlic, partially cover with a lid and cook for 5 minutes, until the leek sweats and softens. Add the tarragon and stir for 1 minute. Add the stock and bring to a boil. Add the artichokes and cook for 10 minutes. Transfer the mixture to a food processor or blender and whizz until smooth. Pour the mixture into a clean saucepan set over low heat and gently reheat. Add the cream, season to taste with salt and pepper, and stir. Ladle the soup into warmed serving bowls, sprinkle with the Roquefort and serve with Pumpkin and Caraway Seed Soda Bread, if liked.

See photograph on page 104.

homemade cheese with roasted baby beets, fennel, and pine nuts

Labneh is a Lebanese soft cheese—it's easy enough to make but you do have to prepare it a day in advance.

a bunch of baby beets (about 12), ends trimmed

4 oz. pine nuts

1 fennel bulb

1 tablespoon freshly squeezed lemon juice

2 garlic cloves, crushed

2 tablespoons olive oil

2 handfuls of mixed baby salad greens

2 scallions, thinly sliced

1 handful of fresh flat-leaf parsley leaves

1 handful of fresh mint leaves

homemade cheese (labneh):

2 cups plain yogurt, preferably sheeps'

1 teaspoon salt

3 tablespoons olive oil

4 small fresh lemon thyme sprigs

1 piece of cheesecloth, 12 inches square

Serves 4

Put the yogurt and salt in a bowl and stir well. Line a strainer with the cheesecloth, put the yogurt into it, fold the cheesecloth up over the top, and set it over a bowl. Refrigerate for 36 hours. The yogurt will drain, leaving a firmer "cheese-like" substance. You can help this process along by giving it a squeeze every few hours. Use 2 spoons to scoop out pieces and put them in a flat dish. Pour over the oil and add the lemon thyme. Cover and chill until needed.

Preheat the oven to 350°F. Put the beets in a roasting tin with 1 cup water and cover with foil. Roast in the preheated oven for 45 minutes, until easily pierced with a skewer. When cool enough to handle, peel off the skins and halve the beets. Put the pine nuts on a baking sheet lined with baking parchment and roast in the still-hot oven for 5 minutes, until just golden. Slice the fennel very thinly and put it in a bowl with half of the lemon juice. Put the garlic, oil, and remaining lemon juice in a separate bowl and whisk to combine. Add the beets, salad greens, scallions, and herbs to the bowl with the fennel, add the dressing and toss. Put the cheese on top and sprinkle with pine nuts to serve.

See photograph on page 105.

chile and garlic steamed mushrooms with polenta

The flavors here are very Italian, but you could easily swap the parsley for coriander, add a splash of light soy sauce and suddenly find yourself in Asia. Almost any cultivated mushroom works here, but do try the recipe with fresh shiitake mushrooms if you decide to go the Asian route.

12 brown mushrooms

¼ cup dry white wine

¼ cup olive oil

2 large red chiles, seeded and chopped

2 garlic cloves, chopped

3 tablespoons finely chopped fresh flat-leaf parsley

crisp polenta:

2 cups whole milk

1 cup instant polenta

1 teaspoon sea salt

5 tablespoons butter

½ cup finely grated Parmesan cheese

1 cup light olive oil

a vegetable steamer, ideally bamboo

Serves 4

Cut any large stalks off the mushrooms and discard. Put the mushroom caps in a non-metallic, flat dish with the wine, oil, chiles, and garlic and use your hands to toss the mushrooms around until coated with the marinade. Cover and let sit for 1 hour.

Sit the dish of mushrooms inside a large steamer, a large Asian bamboo steamer is ideal. Set the steamer over a large saucepan of boiling water, cover, and steam for 20 minutes until tender.

Lightly oil a baking sheet. Put the milk in a saucepan with 2 cups water and set over medium heat. Bring just to a boil, then pour the polenta into the saucepan in a steady stream, whisking constantly to avoid any lumps. Add the salt and stir for 5 minutes until the polenta is soft. Remove from the heat, add the butter and Parmesan, and beat until the mixture is smooth. Spread the polenta out on the oiled baking sheet and put in the refrigerator to chill. When completely cold, cut the polenta into 12 squares. Put the oil in a skillet set over high heat, add the polenta slices and fry for 4–5 minutes on each side until golden and crisp. Remove them from the pan and drain any excess oil on paper towels. Put 3 slices of polenta onto each of 4 serving plates, spoon the mushrooms and juices over the top, and sprinkle with the parsley to serve.

This is my vegetarian take on the classic Spanish rice dish paella. It's colorful, delicious, and bursting with fresh, young vegetables grown on the vine and enhanced with the subtle flavor of saffron. Perfect for summer entertaining.

paella of summer vine vegetables with almonds

a large pinch of saffron threads

⅓ cup olive oil

7 oz. red or yellow cherry tomatoes

4 oz. green beans

4 baby zucchini, halved

3 oz. freshly shelled peas

2 garlic cloves, chopped

2 fresh rosemary sprigs

1½ cups Arborio risotto rice

3½ cups vegetable stock

¼ cup slivered almonds, lightly toasted

Serves 4

Put the saffron in a bowl with ⅓ cup hot water and set aside to infuse. Heat half of the oil in a heavy-based skillet set over high heat and add the tomatoes. Cook for 2 minutes, shaking the skillet so that the tomatoes soften and start to split. Use a slotted spoon to remove the tomatoes from the pan and set aside. Add the beans, zucchini, and peas and stir-fry over high heat for 2–3 minutes. Set aside with the tomatoes until needed.

Add the remaining oil to the large skillet with the garlic and rosemary and cook gently for 1 minute to flavor the oil. Add the rice to the skillet and cook, stirring constantly, for 2 minutes, until the rice is shiny and opaque. Add the stock and saffron water to the skillet. Stir, then increase the heat and let the liquid reach a boil. When the stock is rapidly boiling and little holes have formed in the rice, reduce the heat to medium and let simmer gently for about 20 minutes, until almost all the stock has been absorbed.

Scatter the cooked tomatoes, beans, zucchini, and peas over the rice, cover lightly with some foil and cook over low heat for 5 minutes so that the vegetables are just heated through. Sprinkle the almonds on top to serve.

The trick to this recipe is to take it slowly. I let the red pepper and chiles gently release their color and flavor into the oil by roasting them in a low oven for a full hour. This is contemporary cooking at its best, as it draws on more than one style of cuisine, and it's very much my kind of Saturday night comfort food.

tagliatelle with pan-fried pumpkin and red pepper oil

1 tablespoon light olive oil

14 oz. pumpkin or winter squash, peeled, seeded, and chopped into 1-inch pieces

14 oz. pappardelle, tagliatelle, or any other ribbon pasta

finely grated zest and juice of 1 unwaxed lemon

2 handfuls of arugula

1 large handful of chopped fresh flat-leaf parsley

sea salt and freshly ground black pepper

red pepper oil:

1 small red bell pepper, sliced

6 large red chiles, sliced

1 small red onion, sliced

4 garlic cloves, peeled but left whole

1 teaspoon cumin seeds

¼ cup olive oil

Serves 4

Preheat the oven to 350°F. Put the red bell pepper, chiles, onion, garlic, cumin seeds, and 2 tablespoons of the olive oil in a roasting pan. Cook in the preheated oven for 1 hour, turning often. Transfer the contents of the roasting pan to a food processor while still hot. Add the remaining oil and whizz until smooth. Let cool, then pour the mixture into a clean and dry screwtop jar.

Heat the light olive oil in a skillet set over high and add the pumpkin. Cook for 10 minutes, turning often, until each piece is golden brown all over. Meanwhile, cook the pasta according to the package directions and drain well. Put it in a large bowl and add 2–3 tablespoons of the red pepper oil. Add the cooked pumpkin, lemon zest and juice, arugula, and parsley and toss to combine. Season well with salt and pepper and serve immediately.

Note: The remaining red pepper oil will keep for 1 week when stored in an airtight jar in the fridge. It can be used as a dip for Crispy Oven Wedges (see page 22) or added to tomato-based sauces and soups for extra flavor.

Sometimes we forget how good the simple things can be. I was making a batch of vegetable stock (check out my recipe on page 65). It was early autumn, so I roasted the usual veggie suspects and threw in some whole garlic cloves and thyme sprigs. The tomatoes were overripe and juicy, and when combined with a splash of olive oil the resulting slow-roasted veggies were just too good to make a stock from. A few chickpeas were all that was needed to turn this unassuming sheet of roasted vegetables into a great Saturday dinner. I like to serve them with some Spicy Couscous (see page 103) to soak up the tasty juices.

roasted early autumn vegetables with chickpeas

12 small mushrooms

2 ripe tomatoes, halved

1 red bell pepper, cut into strips

1 yellow bell pepper, cut into strips

1 red onion, cut into wedges

1 small fennel bulb, sliced into thin wedges

1 garlic bulb, broken into individual cloves but left unpeeled

2 teaspoons sea salt

2 tablespoons olive oil

14-oz can chickpeas, drained and rinsed

2 fresh thyme or rosemary sprigs

Spiced Couscous (see page 103), to serve (optional)

Serves 4

Preheat the oven to 350°F. Put the mushrooms, tomatoes, red and yellow bell peppers, onion, fennel, and garlic in a large roasting pan. Sprinkle the salt evenly over the vegetables and drizzle with the oil. Roast in the preheated oven for 1 hour.

Remove the pan from the oven and turn the vegetables. Add the chickpeas and thyme sprigs. Return the pan to the oven and roast for a further 30 minutes, until the edges of the vegetables are just starting to blacken.

To serve, spoon the Spiced Couscous (if using) onto serving plates and top with the warm roasted vegetables with chickpeas.

Stop the presses! This recipe was a last-minute addition to the book. Last summer was a hot one in Australia and I spent most of it outside experimenting on my new barbecue. The marinade here actually started out life as a dressing for a noodle salad from a recipe by the late American food writer Barbara Tropp (who was something of a genius when it came to contemporary Chinese cuisine). I really love it and so was pleased to discover that it also works well as a marinade. You can use pretty much any combination of vegetables that you like, but remember to cook them separately, as it's best not to crowd the grill.

grilled mixed vegetable platter

1 eggplant, thinly sliced
4 brown mushrooms
1 bunch of thin asparagus spears
1 celery rib, cut into ¼-inch lengths
1 red bell pepper, cut into ¾-inch wide strips
vegetable oil, for brushing grill
steamed rice, to serve (optional)

soy balsamic marinade:
½ cup light soy sauce
¼ cup balsamic vinegar
1 tablespoon olive oil
2 teaspoons white sugar

Serves 4

Put all of the ingredients for the marinade in a small bowl and whisk to combine. Arrange the vegetables in a large, non-metallic flat dish and pour over the marinade. Use your hands to toss the vegetables around in the marinade until evenly coated. Cover with plastic wrap and let sit for 1 hour, turning often, to allow the flavors to develop.

Preheat a gas grill to high and brush the grillplate lightly with vegetable oil. Use tongs to transfer the vegetables to a plate and reserve the marinade. Cook the eggplant and mushrooms first, for 2–3 minutes on each side, until dark brown, basting once or twice with a little of the reserved marinade. Transfer to a warmed serving plate. Put the asparagus, celery, and red bell pepper on the grill and cook for 3–4 minutes on each side, basting with a little of the marinade as necessary. Transfer the vegetables to the serving plate with the eggplant and mushrooms.

Serve with steamed rice, if liked. Any remaining marinade can be poured into a small pitcher and used as a sauce.

savory baking

winter vegetable gratin

This is a great way to use up any combination of cold-weather root vegetables, especially those that are often overlooked like rutabaga and my personal favorite parsnip.

7 oz. celeriac, peeled and chopped
1 carrot, peeled and cut into rounds
1 parsnip, peeled and cut into semi-circles
1 small rutabaga, peeled and cut into chunks
2 potatoes, cut into 1-inch pieces
1 cup light cream
1 garlic clove, crushed
1 teaspoon mustard powder
½ cup rye or whole-wheat bread crumbs
2 tablespoons finely grated Parmesan cheese
2 teaspoons fresh marjoram leaves
2 tablespoons butter, melted
sea salt and freshly ground black pepper

Serves 6

Preheat the oven to 350°F and butter a medium ovenproof dish.

Bring a large saucepan of lightly salted water to a boil and add the celeriac, carrot, parsnip, rutabaga, and potatoes. Cook for 10 minutes, drain well, and transfer the vegetables to a large bowl.

Put the cream, garlic, and mustard powder in a small saucepan set over medium heat. Cook, stirring constantly, for about 10 minutes until the mixture is thick and coats the back of a spoon. Season to taste with salt and pepper and pour over the vegetables. Toss well to combine and spoon the mixture into the baking dish.

Put the bread crumbs, Parmesan, and marjoram in a bowl and mix together. Sprinkle the bread crumbs over the vegetables and drizzle the melted butter over the top.

Cook in the preheated oven for about 40 minutes, until the bread crumbs are golden and the mixture around the edge of the baking dish has formed a golden crust.

upside-down bell pepper and tomato pie

It's a very Australian idea to have a tomato-and-onion based veggie fry-up and top it with a rustic dough that could easily be cooked over an open fire (but much easier done in an oven!) I have seen this done with mushrooms, but I think it really needs the juice of the tomatoes to lift it. This makes a great brunch dish for sharing.

2 tablespoons light olive oil
1 small red bell pepper, sliced
2 small red onions, quartered
2 garlic cloves, chopped
14-oz can chopped tomatoes
sea salt and freshly ground black pepper

pastry:
2 cups all-purpose flour
2 teaspoons baking powder
1½ cups grated cheddar cheese
1 teaspoon sea salt
3 tablespoons butter, melted
2 eggs, lightly beaten
¼ cup buttermilk

Serves 6

To make the pastry, put the flour, baking powder, cheese, and salt in the bowl of a food processor. Pulse a couple of times just to combine. Put the melted butter, eggs, and buttermilk in a pitcher and whisk to combine. With the motor of the food processor running, slowly add the egg mixture until the dough becomes sticky. Let sit for 30 minutes while you make the topping.

Preheat the oven to 350°F. Put the oil in a large, nonstick skillet with a heatproof handle and set over high heat. Add the red bell pepper, onions, and garlic and cook for 10 minutes, until the bell pepper slices start to turn golden around the edges. Add the tomatoes, season well with salt and pepper, and cook over high heat for 5 minutes, until almost all the liquid has evaporated from the skillet. Leave the mixture in the skillet and set aside to cool.

Tip the dough onto a lightly floured sheet of baking parchment and form it into a rough circle about the same size as the skillet. Carefully slide the dough onto the tomato mixture in the skillet. Cook in the preheated oven for 20–25 minutes, until the pastry has risen and is light golden. Let cool for a few minutes before turning out onto a serving plate. Cut into slices and serve warm.

See photograph on page 120.

baked spinach mornay

This is really rich and ideally served with something doughy like the Upside-down Bell Pepper and Tomato pie on page 119 or simple salad greens with a tangy vinaigrette. It is also a great brunch dish, perfect with poached eggs and hot, buttered toast.

3 tablespoons butter

2 tablespoons all-purpose flour

3 cups whole milk

7 oz. Fontina cheese, cubed

1 onion, chopped

1 garlic clove, chopped

2 lbs. fresh spinach leaves, chopped

¼ teaspoon freshly grated nutmeg

toasted and buttered sourdough bread, to serve (optional)

Serves 6

Preheat oven to 350°F. Put 2 tablespoons of the butter in a saucepan set over medium heat. When it is melted and sizzling, add the flour and cook for 1 minute, stirring constantly, until a thick paste forms.

Reduce the heat to low and slowly pour the milk into the pan, whisking constantly, until all the milk is incorporated and the mixture is smooth and lump-free. Add the cheese and stir until it has melted into the sauce. Set aside until needed.

Heat the remaining butter in a large skillet set over high heat, add the onion and garlic and cook for 2–3 minutes, until the onion has softened. Add the spinach, cover with a lid, and cook for 4–5 minutes, stirring often, until the spinach has wilted. Transfer the spinach to a large bowl. Pour in the cheese sauce and stir to combine. Spoon the mixture into a large baking dish.

Sprinkle the nutmeg over the top and bake in the preheated oven for 30 minutes until the top of the mornay is golden and bubbling. Serve on slices of toasted and buttered sourdough bread, if liked.

See photograph on page 121.

herbed zucchini and ricotta cheese tart

Phyllo pastry does have a tendency to become a bit soggy, but I have found that cooking this tart in a metal cake pan and sitting it on a preheated baking sheet in the oven goes some way to solving the problem. This is particularly good served with the Greek Salad with Creamy Feta Dressing on page 90.

2 tablespoons olive oil

4–5 zucchini, grated

4 shallots, chopped

1 handful of finely shredded fresh basil leaves

1 handful of finely shredded fresh mint leaves

2 tablespoons finely chopped fresh dill

6 sheets of phyllo pastry, thawed if frozen

3 tablespoons butter, melted

7 oz. fresh ricotta cheese

3 eggs, lightly beaten

¾ cup light cream

8-inch square, nonstick cake pan

Serves 6

Put the oil in a skillet set over high heat. Add the zucchini and cook for 10 minutes, stirring often, until they start to brown. Transfer to a bowl and add the shallots and herbs. Stir to combine and set aside to cool.

Take a sheet of phyllo and lightly brush it all over with some of the melted butter. Fold it in half, brush the top lightly with butter and lay the phyllo in the cake pan, gently pressing it down onto the base and sides. Repeat with the remaining sheets of phyllo, stacking one on top of the other in the pan, until you have used them all. Cover with a clean, damp kitchen towel to keep the pastry moist.

Preheat the oven to 350°F and put a baking sheet on the center shelf of the oven to heat. Put the ricotta, eggs, and cream in a large bowl and add the zucchini mixture. Stir well to combine, then spoon the mixture into the cake pan. Place the pan on the hot baking sheet and bake in the preheated oven for about 30–35 minutes, until the phyllo is golden brown and crisp.

Let the tart cool for 10 minutes before cutting it into squares and serving warm or at room temperature.

I know it's tempting to buy ready-made pastry, but my recipe here is simplicity itself to make and tastes really good. You need not worry about shrinkage either, as leaving it untrimmed looks attractive in a rustic sort of way and ensures that it stays put.

red onion and goat cheese quiche

5 tablespoons butter

4 red onions, thinly sliced

4 eggs, beaten

1¼ cups heavy cream

4 fresh thyme sprigs, roughly chopped

7 oz. soft goat cheese

sea salt and freshly ground black pepper

shortcrust pastry:

1⅓ cups all-purpose flour

1 stick unsalted butter, cubed

1 teaspoon freshly squeezed lemon juice

2–3 tablespoons ice water

a 9-inch diameter ceramic flan dish

Serves 6–8

To make the pastry, put the flour and butter in the bowl of a food processor and put the bowl it in the freezer for 10 minutes. Remove it from the freezer and pulse the ingredients a few times only until they are just combined. With the motor of the food processor running, add the lemon juice and just enough ice water to allow the mixture to form a dough. Do not overbeat it, as this will make the pastry tough. Remove the dough and, using lightly floured hands, form it into a ball. Wrap the ball in plastic wrap and let it rest in the fridge for 30 minutes.

Put the butter in a large saucepan set over high heat. When the butter is sizzling, add the onions and cook them, stirring constantly, for 1 minute. Reduce the heat to medium and gently cook for a further 20–25 minutes, stirring often, until the onions are soft and aromatic. Transfer the onions to a bowl and set aside to cool.

Preheat the oven to 350°F. Roll the pastry out on a sheet of lightly floured baking parchment to form a circle about 12 inches diameter. Use the paper to lift the pastry into the flan dish, gently pressing around the edges to seal. Prick the bottom and sides of the pastry with a fork. Cover the pastry with 2 layers of baking parchment and top with uncooked rice or dried beans. Bake blind in the preheated oven for 15 minutes, until you can see the top of the pastry turning golden. Remove the paper and the rice or beans, brush the pastry shell all over with a little of the beaten egg, and return it to the oven for a further 5 minutes, until the bottom is dry and golden. Remove from the oven and set aside. Leave the oven on

Put the eggs and cream in a bowl and season with salt and pepper. Spoon the onion mixture into the pastry shell. Carefully pour in the egg mixture. Arrange the slices of goat cheese over the top, scatter with the thyme sprigs, and bake in the still-hot oven for about 30 minutes, until the quiche is lightly puffed up and golden. Let cool for 10 minutes before cutting into slices. Serve warm or at room temperature.

In my native Sydney, we are fortunate to have a plethora of excellent Turkish cafés and restaurants serving up fresh baked pide (Turkish bread) alongside colorful and delicious dips. The pide dough is also the base for the Turkish version of pizza, which is often filled or topped with the freshest of vegetables such as tomatoes, spinach, or chard, or tangy feta cheese and sometimes with an egg or two cracked on top before being baked. It's very easy to see where the inspiration for this delicious pie came from!

Swiss chard, feta cheese, and egg pie

3 tablespoons olive oil

2 garlic cloves, sliced

1 red onion, sliced

1 lb. Swiss chard, cut into ¾-inch pieces

4 eggs

7 oz. feta cheese, crumbled

sea salt and freshly ground black pepper

pastry:

2 cups all-purpose flour

1 stick plus 2 tablespoons unsalted butter, cubed

2 egg yolks

2–3 tablespoons ice water

Serves 6

To make the pastry, put the flour and butter in the bowl of a food processor and put the bowl in the freezer for 10 minutes. Pulse the ingredients a few times until just combined. With the motor of the food processor running, add the egg yolks and just enough ice water so that the mixture is on the verge of coming together. Do not overbeat, as this will make the pastry tough. Remove the dough from the bowl and use lightly floured hands to quickly form it into a ball. Wrap in plastic wrap and let rest in the fridge for 30 minutes.

Put 2 tablespoons of the oil in a skillet set over high heat, add the onion and garlic, and cook for 2 minutes, until it softens and just flavors the oil. Add the Swiss chard to the skillet and cook for about 5 minutes, stirring often, until it wilts and softens. Season well with salt and pepper, leave in the skillet and set aside to cool.

Preheat the oven to 425°F. Roll the dough out on a sheet of lightly floured baking parchment to form a circle about 14 inches in diameter, trimming away any uneven bits. Roll the edge over to form a ½-inch border, then roll over again. Transfer the pastry circle to a baking sheet. Spoon the Swiss chard mixture over the pastry. Put the eggs in a bowl and prick the yolks with a fork. Pour the eggs over the Swiss chard so that they are evenly distributed, then scatter the feta over the top. Drizzle the remaining oil over the pie and bake in the preheated oven for about 20 minutes, until the pastry is golden and the top of the pie is just starting to turn brown.

Let cool for 10 minutes before cutting into slices to serve.

Lasagne may well be one of the best-loved of all Italian pasta dishes. Here, mushrooms are combined with Fontina and a creamy béchamel sauce, with mouthwatering results.

wild mushroom lasagne

3 tablespoons butter

1 tablespoon olive oil

1 large white onion, sliced

2 garlic cloves, chopped

2 bay leaves

2¼ lbs. wild mushrooms, sliced

1 cup vegetable stock

1 tablespoon tomato paste

12-oz pack fresh lasagne sheets

3 cups grated Fontina cheese

½ cup finely grated Parmesan cheese

sea salt and freshly ground black pepper

béchamel sauce:

3 tablespoons butter

2 tablespoons all-purpose flour

¼ teaspoon freshly grated nutmeg

3 cups full-fat milk

Serves 8

Put the butter in a saucepan set over medium heat. When the butter sizzles, stir in the flour and nutmeg and cook for 1 minute, stirring constantly. Remove from the heat and pour the milk into the pan, whisking constantly. Return the pan to low heat and cook for 5 minutes, stirring constantly, until the sauce is smooth and creamy.

Preheat the oven to 350°F. Put the butter and oil in a skillet set over high heat and add the onion, garlic, and bay leaves. Cook for 5 minutes until the onion has softened and turned opaque. Add the mushrooms, reduce the heat to medium, and cook for 15 minutes, stirring occasionally, until the mushrooms are evenly cooked. Add the stock and tomato paste and increase the heat to high. Simmer rapidly until the liquid has reduced by half. Season to taste with salt and pepper.

Line the bottom of an oiled baking dish with lasagne sheets. Spread over a third of the sauce. Add one-third each of the mushrooms and grated cheese. Repeat the process and finish with a sheet of lasagne. Spoon over the remaining sauce and sprinkle with Parmesan. Bake in the preheated oven for 45 minutes, until golden brown and bubbling. Leave to rest for 10 minutes before serving.

Here are my favorite pizza toppings, but you can follow this basic pizza dough recipe and top it with whatever seasonal veggies and fresh herbs strike your fancy.

two perfect pizzas

pizza dough:

½ oz. fresh yeast, crumbled

3⅓ cups white bread flour

1 teaspoon sea salt

2 tablespoons fine polenta

cherry tomato, zucchini, and mozzarella:

2 zucchini, thinly sliced

3 tablespoons olive oil

2 garlic cloves, crushed

7 oz. cherry tomatoes

1 large ball of fresh buffalo mozzarella, roughly torn

sea salt and freshly ground black pepper

potato and rosemary:

3 small, new potatoes, very thinly sliced, ideally using a mandoline

2 tablespoons olive oil

2 garlic cloves, chopped

2 tablespoons fresh rosemary needles

sea salt

Each pizza serves 4

To make the dough, put the yeast in a small bowl with ⅓ cup warm water. Stir to break up the yeast, then cover and let sit for 10 minutes, until the mixture looks bubbling and frothy. Put the flour and salt in a food processor and pulse a few times just to combine. Add ½ cup warm water and the yeast mixture and process for a few seconds just to combine. Tip the dough out onto a lightly floured counter and knead it for 10 minutes. Oil the inside of a large bowl and sit the dough in it. Cover with a kitchen towel and let sit in a warm place until it has doubled in size. This will take about 1–1½ hours. Remove the dough from the bowl and punch it down. Divide in half. The dough can be wrapped in plastic wrap and chilled for 3–4 hours before cooking or frozen to use another time.

Sprinkle the polenta on the counter. Take each portion of dough and roll out to either a circle about 10 inches in diameter or a rectangle about 12 x 6 inches, as preferred. Make sure that the dough is less than ¼ inch thick. Preheat the oven to 450°F.

To make the cherry tomato pizza, put the zucchini in a bowl with 2 tablespoons of the oil and the garlic. Season well with salt and pepper. Toss the zucchini around until evenly coated in the garlicky oil. Arrange the zucchini on the pizza base along with the cherry tomatoes. Sprinkle the mozzarella pieces over the top and drizzle with the remaining oil.

To make the potato pizza. Put the potato slices in a bowl with the oil and garlic and season well with salt. Arrange them on the pizza base, scatter with the rosemary needles, and drizzle the garlicky oil from the bowl over the top.

Put 2 baking sheets in the oven for 10–15 minutes, until they are very hot. Carefully transfer the pizzas to the sheets and bake them in the preheated oven for about 20 minutes, until the dough around the edges turns golden. (If your oven is not big enough to take both pizzas side by side, you can cook them on 2 shelves, but do swap them over after 10 minutes of cooking.) Use a spatula to lift them up to check that the bases are cooked golden. Serve immediately.

Focaccia has long been a huge part of the café culture in my hometown of Sydney, where it is served toasted with all sorts of fillings. It's a rustic-style bread at its best, traditionally cooked over an open fire and made for tearing and sharing. If you like this recipe, try it again topped with other ingredients such as red onions, olives, and sprigs of fresh rosemary or thyme.

fennel and tomato focaccia

2 baby fennel bulbs, thinly sliced and fronds chopped

2 tomatoes, thinly sliced

1½ teaspoons sea salt flakes

extra virgin olive oil, to serve

focaccia dough:

3⅓ cups white bread flour

1 teaspoon salt

2 teaspoons dried yeast

3 tablespoons olive oil

all-purpose flour, for kneading and dusting

Serves 6–8

For the dough, sift the flour and salt into a large bowl and add the yeast. Stir to combine and make a small well in the center.

Add 1¼ cups warm water and 2 tablespoons of the olive oil. Quickly stir a few times just to combine, then use your hands to bring the mixture together. (If the mixture is sticking to your hands, add a little flour, but avoid using it if at all possible as adding too much during the kneading process can make the bread chewy.) Transfer the dough to a lightly floured counter and knead for 8–10 minutes, until smooth and elastic. Form the dough into a ball and put it in a lightly oiled bowl. Cover with a kitchen towel and let sit in a warm place for 1½ hours, until doubled in size.

Preheat the oven to 425°F. Put the ball of dough on a lightly oiled baking sheet. Using a lightly floured rolling pin, gently roll from the center upwards in one motion, not pressing too firmly so that any air bubbles stay intact. Roll from the center down to the opposite end to form a rough oval shape, about 12 inches long and 8 inches at its widest point. Lightly cover and let sit again for 20–30 minutes until it has risen.

Use the tips of your fingers to press dimples over the surface of the dough. Lay the fennel and tomato slices on top and scatter with the fronds. Drizzle with the remaining olive oil and sprinkle with the salt flakes. Bake in the preheated oven for 25 minutes. Carefully slide the focaccia off of the sheet and put it directly on the oven shelf. Cook for a further 5 minutes, until the crust is golden. Remove from the oven and let cool before eating. Serve with a small bowl of fruity extra virgin olive oil for dipping.

sweet things

Everyone needs a good chocolate cake recipe, and this could well be the one you've been waiting for! Each time I make this, the texture around the edge of the cake is just a little different to the time before, but it always has the same rich flavor with just a hint of tartness from the raspberries. For best results you will need to start making this the day before you want to eat it and chill overnight.

chocolate and raspberry mousse cake

1½ cups fresh raspberries

14 oz. bittersweet chocolate (no more than 70% cocoa solids), broken up

1 stick plus 7 tablespoons unsalted butter, cubed

6 eggs, separated

¼ cup all-purpose flour

¼ cup superfine sugar

a 9-inch diameter springform cake pan, lightly greased or buttered

an ovenproof plate, large enough to sit on top of the cake pan, wrapped in foil

Serves 10–12

Put the raspberries on a tray or baking sheet lined with baking parchment and put it in the freezer for 2–3 hours. Preheat the oven to 400°F.

Put the chocolate and butter in a large, heatproof bowl and sit the bowl over a saucepan of gently simmering water. (Be careful not to let the bottom of the bowl come into contact with the hot water, as this will spoil the chocolate.) Slowly melt, stirring, until the mixture is smooth and silky, then remove from the heat.

Beat the egg yolks with the flour for 1 minute until thick, making sure there are no lumps. Add to the chocolate mixture and stir well to combine. In a separate, grease-free bowl, beat the egg whites with an electric whisk until they form soft peaks. Sprinkle the sugar over the whites and beat until you have a glossy shine. Use a large metal spoon to fold the egg whites into the chocolate and flour mixture. Do this in 2 batches, working quickly and without overbeating. Add the frozen berries and stir.

Pour the mixture into the cake pan and bake in the preheated oven for 15 minutes. Open the oven, leaving the heat on, and gently sit the foil-wrapped plate on top of the cake pan. Bake for a further 10 minutes. Carefully remove the cake pan from the oven, leaving the plate on top, and let cool completely. When cool, put the cake in the fridge and leave overnight. Remove from the fridge 3 hours before serving so that it comes to room temperature.

Crumbles are normally considered to be a comforting winter dessert, but this deliciously light, nutty version makes the most of juicy summer nectarines. It takes very little time to prepare and tastes sublime with ice cream.

nectarine and pistachio summer crumble

½ cup shelled pistachio nuts, chopped

⅓ cup blanched whole almonds

½ cup oat flour or oatmeal ground in a food processor

4 tablespoons cold unsalted butter, cubed

½ cup all-purpose flour

¼ cup packed brown sugar

6 nectarines

vanilla ice cream or heavy cream, to serve

Serves 6

To make the crumble topping, put the pistachios and almonds in a food processor and process until coarsely chopped. Transfer to a bowl. Add the oat flour and butter and use your fingertips to rub the ingredients together until the mixture resembles coarse, wet sand. Add the all-purpose flour and sugar and rub together to combine. Cover and refrigerate until needed.

Preheat the oven to 425°F. Line a baking sheet with baking parchment. Cut the nectarines in half. If the pit does not come out easily, don't worry—simply slice the flesh off the fruit and drop it directly onto the baking sheet. Sprinkle the crumble topping evenly over the nectarines and bake in the preheated oven for 10–15 minutes, until the fruit is soft and juicy and the topping is a soft golden color. Serve warm with ice cream or heavy cream.

Next time: This crumble works well with any stone fruits so try it with peaches, apricots, or plums.

These are very pretty desserts, perfect for entertaining, as they can be made well in advance and popped in the fridge until you are ready to serve. Note that early forced rhubarb is more tender and will cook much more quickly than the later, ruby-colored stalks. Keep your eye on it as it cooks. You don't want a pink mush, but rather a softly poached fruit that's still intact. I like my custard silky smooth, but if you prefer a thicker custard, simply cook it for a bit longer, until it coats the back of a wooden spoon.

rhubarb and custard pots

10-oz rhubarb, chopped into 1-inch lengths

3 tablespoons superfine sugar

1 teaspoon finely grated orange zest

2 tablespoons freshly squeezed orange juice

custard:

2 cups whipping cream

1 vanilla bean, split in half lengthwise

4 egg yolks

2 tablespoons superfine sugar

2 tablespoons toasted slivered almonds

6 individual serving dishes

Serves 6

Put the rhubarb, sugar, orange zest, and juice in a saucepan with 2 tablespoons water and set over high heat. Cook, stirring occasionally, until the mixture boils. Reduce the heat to medium and simmer for 5 minutes, until the rhubarb is soft but still retains some shape. Spoon the rhubarb into the serving dishes and set aside to cool while you make the custard.

Put the cream in a saucepan. Set over low heat and add the vanilla bean. Slowly bring the cream to a boil. As the cream boils, remove the bean and scrape the seeds into the custard, discarding the bean. Put the egg yolks and sugar in a bowl and whisk for 1 minute. Slowly pour the cream into the yolk mixture, whisking constantly. Transfer the mixture to a clean saucepan and set over low heat. Cook for 5 minutes, being careful not to let it reach a boil.

While still warm, spoon the custard over the rhubarb and let the pots cool in the fridge for at least 3 hours or overnight.

pear and ginger crumble cake

This is a deliciously spicy cake with a very good texture. Note that ground ginger loses its intensity if left sitting in the pantry for too long, so do make sure that what you use it while it's still fragrant. I have made this recipe many times substituting apples for the pears. If you decide to try it with apples, use ground cinnamon instead of the ginger.

8 tablespoons unsalted butter, softened
½ cup plus 2 tablespoons superfine sugar
2 eggs, at room temperature
1 cup all-purpose flour
2 teaspoons baking powder
2 firm pears, peeled, cored, and sliced
1 tablespoon freshly squeezed lemon juice
heavy cream, to serve (optional)

ginger crumble:
½ cup all-purpose flour
1 teaspoon ground ginger
3 tablespoons light brown sugar
3 tablespoons cold unsalted butter, cubed

*a 9-inch diameter springform cake pan,
lined with baking parchment and greased*

To make the crumble mixture, put the flour and ginger in a large bowl. Add the cold butter and quickly rub it into the flour using your fingertips. Add the sugar and rub again until the mixture resembles coarse sand. Refrigerate until needed.

Preheat the oven to 350°F. Beat the softened butter and sugar with an electric whisk until pale and creamy. Add the eggs, 1 at a time, and beat well between each addition. Tip in the flour and baking powder and beat for 1 minute, until the mixture is smooth and well combined. Pour it into the prepared cake pan. Toss the pears in a bowl with the lemon juice and put them on top of the cake. Sprinkle the crumble topping over the top and bake in the preheated oven for 40–45 minutes, until the cake is golden on top.

Let cool slightly before removing from the pan and serving warm with heavy cream, if liked.

upside-down peach cake

You can use either yellow or white peaches here. I prefer the more robust flavor of yellow peaches—the white ones have a more subtle flavor that is more like that of nectarines, which are, after all, peaches without the fuzzy skin. Look out for locally grown, market-fresh, juicy summer peaches and try to resist eating them before you make this delicious cake!

4 large peaches
1 stick unsalted butter, softened
1 scant cup packed brown sugar
3 eggs, separated
¾ cup plus 2 tablespoons self-rising flour
1 cup sour cream
confectioners' sugar, for dusting
light cream, to serve (optional)

*a 9-inch diameter springform cake pan, lined
with baking parchment and greased*

Preheat the oven to 350°F. Halve the peaches, discard the pit, then cut each half in half again. Arrange the peach quarters on the bottom of the cake pan and set aside while making the cake batter.

Put the butter and sugar in a large bowl and beat with an electric whisk until the sugar has completely dissolved and the mixture is the colour of caramel. Add the egg yolks, 1 at a time, beating for 1 minute between each addition. Fold the flour and sour cream through in 2 batches.

In a separate grease-free bowl, beat the egg whites with an electric whisk until they form firm peaks. Using a large metal spoon, fold the whites into the cake batter in 2 batches. Spoon the mixture over the peaches and bake in the preheated oven for 40–45 minutes, until the top of the cake is golden and the center springs back when gently pressed.

Let cool for 10 minutes before carefully turning out onto a serving plate. Dust with confectioners' sugar and serve warm with light cream for pouring, if liked.

See photograph on page 144.

almond and lemon cake

Lemons and almonds are a flavor match made in heaven. It is all too easy to buy almonds pre-ground in packets, but by the time they reach you they have lost much of their flavor. Grinding your own only takes a few minutes and the almond oil in the nuts is slowly released as the cake bakes in the hot oven to give a full and rich flavor. This cake is delicious eaten warm from the oven for afternoon tea or served with some vanilla ice cream as a dessert.

1 cup blanched whole almonds

3 unwaxed lemons

1 stick plus 6 tablespoons butter

⅔ cup superfine sugar

3 eggs

½ cup all-purpose flour

1 teaspoon baking powder

lemon icing:

⅔ cup confectioners' sugar

2 tablespoons freshly squeezed lemon juice

a 8-inch square cake pan, lined with baking parchment and greased

Serves 8–10

Preheat the oven to 350°F. Put the almonds on a baking sheet and toast in the preheated oven for 5 minutes, until aromatic and just starting to turn golden. Let cool, then transfer to a food processor. Process the nuts until finely chopped and set aside until needed.

Finely grate the zest from 2 of the lemons and squeeze all 3 of them so that you have ⅓ cup lemon juice. Put the butter, superfine sugar, and lemon zest in a bowl and, using an electric whisk, beat for about 5 minutes, until the mixture is thick. Add the eggs, 1 at a time, and beat well between each addition. Fold in the flour, baking powder, and ground almonds. Add the lemon juice and stir to combine. Spoon the mixture into the prepared pan and bake in the preheated oven for about 35 minutes, until the top of the cake is golden and the center springs back when gently pressed. Remove from the pan and let cool.

To make the icing, beat the confectioners' sugar with the lemon juice for 2 minutes. Drizzle the icing over the cake and let set before serving.

See photograph on page 145.

carrot and walnut cake with cream cheese frosting

Carrot cake began its life as a hippy cake in the '70s and was then mass produced for the booming Sydney café scene in the '80s. My version is crumbly and soft and probably best eaten with a spoon. If you are nervous about cutting the cake through the center, simply spread the frosting over the top of the cooled cake instead.

2 eggs, separated

½ cup plus 1 tablespoon raw sugar

¾ cup plus 1 tablespoon light olive oil

1 teaspoon baking soda

¾ cup plus 2 tablespoons all-purpose flour

2 teaspoons baking powder

1 teaspoon ground cinnamon

¼ teaspoon freshly grated nutmeg

1 cup grated carrot

⅓ cup walnut halves

cream cheese frosting:

8 oz. cream cheese

1 stick butter, cubed

3 tablespoons brown sugar

2–3 tablespoons pure maple syrup

a 7-inch diameter springform cake pan, lightly greased

Serves 8

Put the egg yolks and sugar in a large bowl and beat for 2 minutes. Add the oil and baking soda and beat until just combined. Fold in the flour, spices, carrot, and walnuts until combined. The mixture should look quite thick. In a separate grease-free bowl, beat the egg whites with an electric whisk until they form soft peaks then fold them into the cake batter in 2 batches. Spoon the cake batter into the prepared cake pan and bake for 45–50 minutes, until golden and slightly puffed on top. Let the cake cool in the pan for about 10 minutes before turning it out onto a wire rack.

To make the frosting, put the cream cheese and butter in a bowl and let them come to room temperature. Add the brown sugar and, using an electric whisk, beat for 5 minutes, until there are no lumps and the beaters leave a trail when turned off. Add the maple syrup a little at a time and beat for a further 2 minutes, until the mixture is smooth and a spreadable consistency. Carefully slice the cooled cake in half and spread the frosting on the bottom layer.

cherry and ricotta strudel

This fruit-filled strudel is, like the carrot cake on page 146, just a little bit retro, but I think some things do enough time in culinary purgatory to warrant a comeback! Fresh ricotta cheese is combined with summer-ripe cherries and crispy phyllo with great success. Best of all, you can make this in advance and freeze it. There is no need to thaw before cooking—just give it a little more time in the oven. You could try using sliced green apples instead of the cherries.

1 lb. fresh cherries, pitted
⅓ cup confectioners' sugar, plus extra
for dusting
2 teaspoons cornstarch
8 sheets of phyllo pastry, thawed if frozen
⅔ cup ground almonds (pre-packaged or
see Almond and Lemon Cake on page 146)
5 oz. fresh ricotta cheese
5 tablespoons unsalted butter, melted

Serves 8

Put the cherries, 1 tablespoon of the confectioners' sugar and the cornstarch in a bowl and let sit for 30 minutes, stirring often. Preheat the oven to 425°F.

Put the ground almonds and 2 tablepoons of the remaining confectioners' sugar in a bowl and mix to combine. Put the ricotta in a separate bowl, add the remaining confectioners' sugar and mix to combine. Set aside until needed. Put a baking sheet in the preheated oven to heat up. (This will prevent the bottom of the phyllo becoming soggy.)

Put a sheet of baking parchment on a work bench. Lay a sheet of phyllo on the baking parchment, longest edge nearest to you. Brush all over with melted butter until the phyllo is shiny. Sprinkle 1–2 tablespoons of the ground almond mixture over the pastry. Repeat with the remaining sheets of phyllo, butter, and almond mixture, finishing with the final sheet of phyllo.

Working quickly, so that the phyllo does not become soggy, spread the ricotta mixture over the pastry, leaving a 2-inch margin around the edges. Spoon the cherry mixture over the top. Fold the edge nearest to you up and over the filling, tucking in the shorter edges as you roll. Make sure the strudel is sitting seam-side down. Use the baking parchment to lift the strudel onto the hot baking sheet. Bake in the preheated oven for 12–15 minutes, until golden brown.

Remove from the oven and let cool slightly before dusting liberally with confectioners' sugar and cutting into slices to serve.

fresh fig and walnut meringue

Maggie Beer is a popular character in the Australian food scene and she is a passionate advocate of farm-fresh produce. The inspiration for this meringue comes from one of her recipes, but she uses dried figs rather than fresh. Don't use big figs here, as they will split and prevent the egg whites from cooking and the meringue will become sloppy. I found some small, very black ones that were perfect with the caramelly meringue.

1 cup walnut halves
8–10 small black fresh figs, halved
6 large egg whites
1¼ cups packed brown sugar

an 8-inch diameter circle of baking parchment

Serves 8–10

Preheat the oven to 350°F. Put the walnuts on a baking sheet and toast in the preheated oven for 5 minutes, until just starting to turn golden. Remove and let cool. Leave the oven on.

Put the egg whites in a large, grease-free bowl and beat with an electric whisk until they form soft peaks. Add a tablespoon of the sugar at a time, beating well between each addition, and continue until all the sugar has been added and the meringue resembles a thick, fluffy caramel. Add the figs and walnuts and stir to combine.

Put the circle of baking parchment on a baking sheet. Use a spoon to transfer the mixture onto the paper, keeping within the circle and using the back of the spoon to create dents and peaks for a rustic effect. Bake in the preheated oven for 40–45 minutes, until the peaks of the meringue are a dark golden color.

Let cool for 15 minutes then slide a large knife under the meringue to remove it from the paper and transfer it to a serving plate. This is best eaten warm or a room temperature.

See photograph on page 150.

strawberry meringue roulade

I love meringues, but I am not too fond of the pressure to make the conventional "perfect" meringue. I'm all for messy recipes—those that you actually want to eat, not those that you're afraid to touch! It doesn't matter if this meringue splits or isn't crispy; it's not meant to be. It's really just an excuse to eat lots of fresh strawberries and cream. Simple.

3 egg whites
1 teaspoon cornstarch
¾ cup superfine sugar, plus 2 teaspoons
½ cup whipping cream
3 tablespoons confectioners' sugar, plus extra for dusting
2 cups fresh strawberries, hulled and sliced

Serves 4–6

Preheat the oven to 250°F. Line a baking sheet with baking parchment and sprinkle over 1 teaspoon superfine sugar. (This will stop the meringue from sticking.)

Put the egg whites in a grease-free bowl, add the cornstarch and beat with an electric whisk until soft peaks form. Add 1 tablespoon of sugar at a time, beating well between each addition, and continue beating until you can no longer feel grains of sugar when you rub the mixture between your thumb and forefinger. Use a large metal spoon to transfer the mixture to the prepared baking sheet and smooth it out with a palette knife. You want a rectangle about 8 x 12 inches cm and no thicker than ½ inch. Bake the meringue in the preheated oven for 20 minutes, until it is just set and the top turns a light caramel color and is not sticky when lightly touched.

Take a second piece of baking parchment, slightly larger than the meringue, and sprinkle over 1 teaspoon superfine sugar. Quickly flip the sheet upside-down so that the meringue is turned out onto the paper. Tap the bottom of the sheet so that the meringue comes away in one piece. Peel off the bottom piece of baking parchment. Firmly roll the meringue up into a log with the second sheet of paper and wrap in a clean kitchen towel. Set aside to cool completely.

Put the cream and confectioners' sugar in a bowl and whisk until firm peaks form. Unroll the meringue. Spoon the cream over the meringue, leaving a 1-inch margin around the edge. Arrange the sliced strawberries over the cream and roll up. Dust liberally with confectioners' sugar and cut into thick slices to serve.

See photograph on page 151.

coconut creamed rice with poached plums

Canned coconut milk is a must-have pantry staple for me, as I use it in lots of dishes, both savory and sweet. This is a particular favorite. At the market, choose a sweet, large variety of plum for poaching and pick fruits with a silvery patina, as it's an indicator of freshness. The coconut creamed rice is also lovely with softly poached cherries.

8 plums, halved and pitted
½ cup raw sugar
1 cinnamon stick
2 green cardamom pods

creamed coconut rice:
½ cup short-grain rice
2 x 14-oz cans coconut milk
½ cup superfine sugar
½ cup whipping cream

Serves 6

To make the coconut creamed rice, put the rice in a strainer and rinse it under cold running water until the water runs clear. Drain well. Put the rice in a large saucepan set over high heat and add the coconut milk and sugar. Bring to a gentle boil, then reduce the heat to low and cook for 25–30 minutes, stirring often to ensure that the rice doesn't catch. Let cool. Whip the cream until soft peaks form, then fold it into the rice mixture.

Meanwhile, put the plums, sugar, cinnamon stick, and cardamom pods in a saucepan and add 1 cup water. Bring to a boil, then reduce heat to low and cook for 20 minutes, gently turning the plums often, until they soften but retain their shape. Remove the cinnamon stick and cardamom pods from the pan.

Divide the creamed rice between serving dishes and spoon the warm plums over the top. Serve immediately.

Granny Smith apples were first cultivated in my hometown of Sydney by Maria Ann Smith (aka Granny!) I suppose she saw their potential as a good all-round cooking apple. Their flesh collapses when cooked, making them perfect for apple sauce. I like them in sweet desserts, such as this self-saucing one, but they are not ideal for tarts and cakes. I've used mild, sweet blueberries here as they are widely available, but if you find mulberries (truly seasonal and rarely grown commercially), don't hesitate to use them in this pudding.

baked Granny Smith and blueberry pudding

2 tart green apples, such as Granny Smith

1 cup blueberries

1 cup all-purpose flour

3 teaspoons baking powder

½ cup plus 2 tablespoons superfine sugar

1 cup buttermilk

1 egg

1 vanilla bean

½ cup packed brown sugar

light cream, to serve (optional)

Serves 6

Preheat the oven to 350°F and generously butter a medium baking dish. Peel and core the apples then thinly slice them directly into the baking dish, arranging them in the bottom of the dish with the blueberries.

Sift the flour, baking powder, and superfine sugar into a large bowl. Put the buttermilk and egg in a separate bowl. Split the vanilla bean in half lengthwise and scrape the seeds from the bean directly into this bowl, then stir to combine. Pour the buttermilk mixture into the flour mixture and beat well to combine.

Pour the mixture over the fruit in the baking dish. Working quickly, put the brown sugar in a pitcher and add 1 cup boiling water. Stir until the sugar has dissolved. Carefully pour it into the baking dish, pouring into a corner. Bake the pudding in the preheated oven for 45 minutes, until the surface feels dry and springs back when lightly touched. Serve warm with light cream for pouring, if liked.

This is an impressive pudding for relatively little work. The sweet and buttery brioche works well with the tangy blackberries. Try and buy very sweet blackberries for this, as they will be softer and juicier, which is exactly what you want here. The dark purple juices should bleed into the pudding to create a pretty, marbled effect.

baked brioche pudding with blackberries

4 brioche rolls or ½ 14-oz brioche loaf

3 tablespoons butter, softened

2 cups fresh blackberries

3 eggs

½ cup heavy cream

1½ cups whole milk

⅓ cup superfine sugar

2 tablespoons raw sugar

vanilla ice cream, to serve (optional)

Serves 6

Slice the brioche to give you 6–8 thin slices. Lightly butter the slices on one side and arrange them in the bottom of a medium baking dish, overlapping them slightly. Put half the blackberries on top. Repeat with the remaining brioche slices and blackberries. Put the cream, eggs, milk, and superfine sugar in a bowl or pitcher and beat to combine. Pour the mixture over the brioche in the baking dish. Cover with foil and let sit for 30 minutes to allow the brioche to absorb the liquid.

Preheat the oven to 350°F. Sprinkle the raw sugar over the top of the pudding and bake it in the preheated oven for 40–45 minutes, until the top of the pudding is golden brown. Serve warm with vanilla ice cream, if liked.

websites and mail order

where to buy fresh produce

www.ams.usda.gov/farmersmarkets
Farmers' markets hotline at:
1-800-384-8704
To find a farmers' market in your state, check out the list compiled by the US Department of Agriculture.

www.localharvest.org
Use this site to find farmers' markets, family farms, and other sources of sustainably grown food in your area. Includes information on where you can buy fresh produce. Features a complete A-Z listing of farmers' markets in the US.

www.csacenter.org
Provides complete information on Community Supported Agriculture (CSA) operations in your area. This is a way for the food-buying public to create a relationship with a local farm and receive a weekly basket of produce. By making a financial commitment to a farm, people become "members" of the CSA.

www.foodroutes.org
Food Routes provides information about local markets, and Community Supported Agriculture farms (see above).

www.eatwellguide.org
The Eat Well Guide is a list of sustainable food resources including farms, markets, and restaurants in the US and Canada.

food markets

www.cenyc.org
CENYC, the Council on the Environment of New York City, sponsors several farmers' markets throughout the city. Visit their site for market schedules and maps.

www.williamsburgfarmersmarket.com
Historic Williamsburg hosts a hip, happening farmers' market on Tuesdays and Saturdays.

www.madfarmmkt.org
The Dane County farmers' market takes place on the State Capitol Square every Saturday in Madison, Wisconsin.

www.wholefoodsmarket.com
Whole Foods Market is the world's largest retailer of natural and organic foods, with more than 140 stores across the US and Canada.

home delivery and mail order

www.localharvest.org
Over 4,500 products available to buy on-line including local produce, fruits, dairy, eggs, and heirloom seeds.

www.diamondorganics.com
Fresh all-organic food, with guaranteed nationwide overnight home delivery in Canada.

www.greenearthorganics.com
Organic food home delivery service with delivers pesticide free, naturally-grown organic produce.

www.doortodoorganics.com
The East Coast's premier source of fresh organic produce since 1996. Delivery of farm fresh organic vegetables and fruits to your home or office.

www.seedsofchange.com
For certified organic and heirloom vegetable seeds and fruit trees available by mail order.

interesting food-related organizations

www.navs-online.org
The North American vegetarian society is a non-profit educational organization dedicated to promoting the vegetarian way of life. Since its inception in 1974, it has organized and sponsored annual vegetarian conferences including two world events.

www.organicconsumers.org
Campaigning for "health, justice, and sustainability." Find local food news, events, and green businesses on state pages plus information about the "buy local" movement.

conversion charts

Weights and measures have been rounded up or down slightly to make measuring easier.

1 stick butter	8 tablespoons	125 g

Volume equivalents:

American	Metric	Imperial
1 teaspoon	5 ml	
1 tablespoon	15 ml	
¼ cup	60 ml	2 fl.oz.
⅓ cup	75 ml	2½ fl.oz.
½ cup	125 ml	4 fl.oz.
⅔ cup	150 ml	5 fl.oz. (¼ pint)
¾ cup	175 ml	6 fl.oz.
1 cup	250 ml	8 fl.oz.

Weight equivalents:

Imperial	Metric
1 oz.	25 g
2 oz.	50 g
3 oz.	75 g
4 oz.	125 g
5 oz.	150 g
6 oz.	175 g
7 oz.	200 g
8 oz. (½ lb.)	250 g
9 oz.	275 g
10 oz.	300 g
11 oz.	325 g
12 oz.	375 g
13 oz.	400 g
14 oz.	425 g
15 oz.	475 g
16 oz. (1 lb.)	500 g
2 lb.	1 kg

Measurements:

Inches	Cm
¼ inch	5 mm
½ inch	1 cm
¾ inch	1.5 cm
1 inch	2.5 cm
2 inches	5 cm
3 inches	7 cm
4 inches	10 cm
5 inches	12 cm
6 inches	15 cm
7 inches	18 cm
8 inches	20 cm
9 inches	23 cm
10 inches	25 cm
11 inches	28 cm
12 inches	30 cm

Oven temperatures:

110°C	(225°F)	Gas ¼
120°C	(250°F)	Gas ½
140°C	(275°F)	Gas 1
150°C	(300°F)	Gas 2
160°C	(325°F)	Gas 3
180°C	(350°F)	Gas 4
190°C	(375°F)	Gas 5
200°C	(400°F)	Gas 6
220°C	(425°F)	Gas 7
230°C	(450°F)	Gas 8
240°C	(475°F)	Gas 9

index